100

THINGS TO DO IN
COLUMBUS
BEFORE YOU
DIE

2nd Edition

2nd Edition

100

THINGS TO DO IN
COLUMBUS
BEFORE YOU
DIE

● ●

ANIETRA HAMPER

REEDY PRESS

Library of Congress Control Number: 2018962611

ISBN: 9781681062006

Design by Jill Halpin

Printed in the United States of America
19 20 21 22 23   5 4 3 2 1

Please note that websites, phone numbers, addresses, and company names are subject to change or cancellation. We did our best to relay the most accurate information available, but due to circumstances beyond our control, please do not hold us liable for misinformation. When exploring new destinations, please do your homework before you go.

DEDICATION

To my older brothers, Shay and Keir, who taught me during our childhood that the true joy in finding cool things to do starts with insight from personal exploration and ends with finding ways to make those experiences uniquely your own.

CONTENTS

• •

Music and Entertainment

● ●

• •

PREFACE

As a Columbus native, it is inspiring to see my hometown growing and thriving as the fifteenth-largest city in the United States and the fastest-growing city in Ohio. I spent most of my television news career in Columbus, and I am fortunate that it is now the home base for my business.

Columbus is a fascinating mix of the traditional and the innovative, highlighting Midwestern values and warmth while encouraging new kinds of experiences in art, food, fashion, entertainment, sports, and business. For example, the COSI electrostatic generator which seemed like the ultimate sci fi experience to me as a child is part of a larger experience to be had at the riverfront science complex. I remember having my first scoop of Jeni's ice cream at a small North Market vendor stall long before it became an international brand. As a reporter, I remember covering the news conferences announcing that Columbus was getting both NHL hockey and MLS soccer teams that would place us in the professional sports spotlight.

Not much has changed in Columbus since my youth, yet everything has changed. Columbus is a city that embraces its past by showcasing its agricultural roots and investing in historic preservation. But the city also stands proudly on the forefront of modern development with an expanding downtown riverfront and resources that continue to attract large companies that build their headquarters in Columbus and its suburbs.

• •

So, go ahead and indulge in a citywide festival like the Red, White and Boom Independence Day celebration with eight hundred thousand Columbusites gathering on the downtown streets, sit for quiet reflection at the National Veterans Memorial and Museum, go for a belly laugh at Shadowbox Live with cabaret-style entertainment, cheer on the Columbus Blue Jackets NHL team, delight in the thrill of a discounted fashion find, discover new intellect at the Columbus Museum of Art, select a basket of fresh produce at a farmers market, or sip a craft cocktail at a modern-day speakeasy.

While selecting only one hundred of the best establishments and experiences in Columbus hardly seems fair, I hope you will use this book as a starting point to explore and find your own best experiences in the city. Columbus is the kind of city where happy surprises can be found in every corner, and that's something we can all use.

ACKNOWLEDGMENTS

I would like to thank my parents, Don and Roberta, my loving family, Jeffery Stallings, Experience Columbus, local business owners, many community partners, and the wonderful people of Columbus who made this book possible.

FOOD AND DRINK

REVEL IN SWEET TOOTH SATISFACTION:
EXPERIENCE ARTISANAL ICE CREAM AT ITS BEST

Ohio has deep roots in the dairy industry, so Columbus takes ice cream seriously. Jump into the line at any one of the Jeni's Splendid Ice Creams locations for an artisanal double scoop of Ricotta Toast with Red Berry Geranium Jam or Queen City Cayenne Chocolate. Jeni's is a hometown favorite with national fame known for using fresh natural ingredients sourced directly from the farms where they are produced. Jeni's humble beginnings started in the North Market where they still sell ice cream today. Another hometown favorite, Graeter's, offers tours of its factory sharing the inside scoop on how French Pot freezers create popular flavors like Black Raspberry Chocolate Chip and the Danish pastry–inspired Cheese Crown. Johnson's Real Ice Cream in Bexley serves up a traditional scoop shop experience with more than fifty flavor options, and Whit's Frozen Custard is tops for a non–ice cream alternative with flavors that change weekly.

Jeni's Splendid Ice Creams
59 Spruce St. in the North Market/various locations,
(614) 228-9960
jenis.com

Graeter's
Various locations
graeters.com/neighborhood-locations

Johnson's Real Ice Cream
2728 E. Main St. in Bexley, (614) 231-0014
55 W. Bridge St. in Dublin, (614) 328-5827
160 W. Main St. in New Albany, (614) 924-7744
johnsonsrealicecream.com

Whit's Frozen Custard
Various locations
whitscustard.com

STROLL LOCAL VENDOR STALLS
AT THE NORTH MARKET

The North Market in the heart of downtown Columbus is a social and culinary hub where local vendors sell a variety of products from fresh meat and seafood to spices, flowers, donuts, and craft beer. The market is open every day of the week, but the Saturday morning and summer night markets are especially enjoyable. The historic two-story brick warehouse has more than thirty vendor stalls and eateries showcasing food from around the world. Pick up some macaroons from Pistacia Vera or locally made hot sauces ranging from mild to ghost-pepper hot at Flavor & Fire. Food vendors are busy at lunchtime serving authentic Polish sausage from Hubert's Polish Kitchen, pho from Lan Viet Market, vegan dishes at Flavors of India, and fried chicken with cayenne-infused sauce at Hot Chicken Takeover. If you are looking to embrace the local food scene, the North Market is the place to start.

North Market
59 Spruce St., (614) 463-9664
northmarket.com

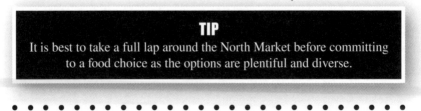

TIP
It is best to take a full lap around the North Market before committing to a food choice as the options are plentiful and diverse.

JOIN
THE FOOD TRUCK FUN

The food truck phenomenon is thriving in Columbus with pop-up eateries featuring everything from gourmet grilled cheese to mountainous nachos at festivals, charity events, and on street corners at lunchtime. The best bet for sampling some of the top food truck fare in Columbus is during the annual three-day Columbus Food Truck Festival held every August at the Columbus Commons. But, every day more than two hundred food trucks zoom around the city ready to satisfy taste buds and offer up food that fits whatever moods strike their hungry patrons. Foodies can download an app and search the Central Ohio Food Truck Association website for real-time truck locations. Try some Korean kimbap from the Ajumama truck, comfort food like Alphabetical soup from Alphabetical, or all-day breakfast from the Broke Johnny Food Truck. In the mood for soul food? Go for the Shrimp Po Boy Basket from M & S Grub Hub or go vegan at Kinetic.

Central Ohio Food Truck Association
centralohiofoodtruck.org

Columbus Food Truck Festival
columbusfoodtruckfest.com

GET ETHNIC
THROUGH YOUR TASTE BUDS

The ethnic food scene in Columbus is exploding with restaurants that represent more than forty nationalities and are growing by the day. One of the best ways to sample Columbus's diverse ethnic food options is on the Alt Eats Food Tour hosted by Columbus Food Adventures. It is a fun way to sample many types of international food in one experience. The tour heads to the heart of one of the largest immigrant communities in Columbus near Cleveland Avenue to sample Somali, Nigerian, and Mexican cuisine. Columbus is an immigration melting pot and has been since its early years when German settlers moved into the south side. The ethnic eats in Columbus range from German and Italian to Indian, Vietnamese, and Salvadorian cuisine. Ethnic eats are popping up in nearly every neighborhood and suburb around Columbus. Don't know where to start? Check out the following website.

Columbus Food Adventures
columbusfoodadventures.com

INDULGE IN A FAMOUS CREAM PUFF
AT SCHMIDT'S SAUSAGE HAUS

Schmidt's Sausage Haus und Restaurant in German Village is a culinary institution in Columbus with fans who never fail to wrap up every delicious meal with Schmidt's famous cream puff. It began its rise to tasty fame when the Schmidt family joined Columbus's German settlers in the 1880s and opened a meat packing business. Schmidt's restaurant opened in 1967 serving fresh meat dishes and original dessert recipes from the homeland, including the decadent cream puff, a half-pound concoction of delicate pastry filled with specially whipped cream, flavored with your choice of vanilla, chocolate, or peanut butter. It is tough to save room for the cream puff after a meal of sauerkraut-bratwurst balls or the famous Bahama Mama® sausage, but it's worth a try. There is usually a wait at the restaurant, so go early as it is always busy and they do not take reservations.

Schmidt's Sausage Haus und Restaurant
240 E. Kossuth St., (614) 444-6808
schmidthaus.com

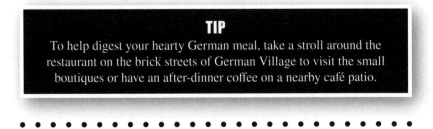

TIP
To help digest your hearty German meal, take a stroll around the restaurant on the brick streets of German Village to visit the small boutiques or have an after-dinner coffee on a nearby café patio.

GO A LITTLE NUTTY
AT THE KREMA NUT COMPANY

The Krema Nut Company is one of the best-kept secret food gems in Columbus and one of the oldest peanut butter manufacturing companies in the United States. For more than a century the Krema Nut Company has produced gourmet nuts roasted in small batches and natural peanut butter with no preservatives, salt, or sugar. What's more impressive is the company's fancied-up traditional peanut butter sandwiches. Specialty PB&J offerings include the "Buckeye" PB&J featuring Krema's fresh ground natural peanut butter and Nutella chocolate hazelnut spread. Another favorite is the Nutty Mallow featuring fresh natural peanut butter paired with oozing marshmallow fluff competing for space between the slices of Great Harvest bread. Stop by the flagship store and factory to pick up a few sandwiches (and maybe even a PB&J ice cream sundae) and take lunch to a new level.

Krema Nut Company
1000 W. Goodale Blvd., (614) 299-4131
krema.com

EAT STEAK THE OLD-FASHIONED WAY
AT THE TOP

Not much has changed since 1955 at the Top steakhouse in Bexley. The supper club restaurant is a Columbus institution known as much for its perfectly cooked charbroiled steaks and olive-studded gin martinis as for its dimly lit, lounge-style atmosphere. The original wood-paneled dining room, low ceilings, and leather booths take hungry patrons on a time-travel odyssey to an era when steaks came with bragging rights. The original piano bar still features nightly entertainment, setting the mood for the milestones that are often celebrated at the Top like birthdays and anniversaries. For a truly special dinner, order the most popular steak on the menu, a twenty-four-ounce USDA Prime Bone-in Ribeye dry aged for thirty-five days or a jumbo lobster tail. If the decision is too tough, then go for the surf and turf.

The Top
2891 E. Main St. in Bexley, (614) 231-8238
thetopsteakhouse.com

SAVOR A CANDY BUCKEYE
AT THE ANTHONY-THOMAS
CANDY FACTORY

It is difficult to visit Columbus and NOT be gifted with a buckeye nut for good luck, see a buckeye tree (the state tree of Ohio), cheer on the OSU Buckeyes, or indulge in the decadent candy buckeye. Fortunately for Columbus, the Anthony-Thomas Candy Company is based in the city and is always at the ready with boxes of buckeyes to go. The peanut butter and chocolate candies are so decadent that it is nearly impossible to have just one. It's okay, they are small, so go ahead and indulge. The Anthony-Thomas Candy retail stores located throughout the city often have buckeye samples readily available. The ultimate way to experience the candy buckeye is by taking a tour through the Anthony-Thomas Candy factory. The free tours offer a close-up view of the effort that goes into cranking out thirty thousand pounds of chocolate per shift.

Anthony-Thomas Candy Company
1777 Arlingate Ln., (614) 272-9221
Various locations
anthony-thomas.com

SAMPLE HOT NUTS
FROM A VINTAGE PEANUT ROASTER
AT THE PEANUT SHOPPE

Conjure up some nostalgia with a handful of hot cashews from the Peanut Shoppe in downtown Columbus. The old-fashioned peanut shop has remained a staple around Capitol Square for more than eighty-three years, delighting downtown workers and passers-by with the wafting aroma of fresh nuts, roasted daily. The original peanut roaster and vintage Mr. Peanut sculpture riding on top of it inside the front door date back to the early 1900s. Shout out, "What's hot?" when you walk in the front door to find out what's churning in the roaster that day. It could be hot cashews, peanuts, walnuts, hazelnuts, or Spanish peanuts. The nostalgic infusion continues inside the candy counters with old-fashioned candy options from spice drops to maple nut goodies. For those who enjoy antiques, the tiny shop features one-of-a-kind Planters Peanuts memorabilia, including the neon sign hanging outside, which is the only original one still used.

The Peanut Shoppe
21 E. State St., (614) 221-8837

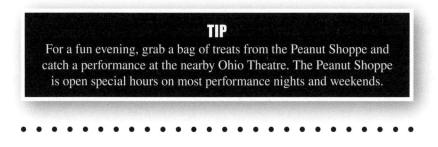

TIP
For a fun evening, grab a bag of treats from the Peanut Shoppe and catch a performance at the nearby Ohio Theatre. The Peanut Shoppe is open special hours on most performance nights and weekends.

THROW A "PAWTIE" FOR FIDO
AT BREWDOG

Columbus has such a vibrant foodie and brewery scene that now even dogs can log some social time while their owners indulge. The BrewDog USA headquarters and brewery in Canal Winchester now allows pet owners to throw a birthday "pawtie" for their dogs in an outdoor dog park attached to the brewery. But the cool factor for Fido doesn't end there. The "pawtie" invites can be extended to all of the guest of honor's dog friends for $10 a head. Four-legged guests get a dog-safe birthday cake prepared by a local bakery and even dog beer, a special brew from the taproom made from boiled carrots and bananas. The BrewDog brewery and taproom features craft beers and a gaming area with pinball machines. There is even a hotel at the brewery, the DogHouse, the world's first crowdfunded craft beer hotel. The UK craft beer makers have made Columbus their U.S. headquarters, with three locations in the city.

BrewDog
96 Gender Rd. in Canal Winchester, (614) 908-3051
brewdog.com

Credit: BrewDog

FILL A BASKET
AT A FARMERS MARKET

One of the most splendid joys of summer in and around Columbus is hitting the farmers markets that take place almost daily and in nearly every neighborhood, featuring fresh Ohio produce. Celebrate Ohio's agricultural roots by filling a basket with just-picked vine-ripe tomatoes, Ohio sweet corn, peaches, meats, and cheese. Fresh out of the ground, the just-harvested green beans and carrots will enhance any dish to which they are added. Local farmers markets are great destination points even if you are not looking for produce. Many have entertainment, children's activities, and other goods for sale. The North Market hosts the oldest and largest farmers market from June through October on summer weekends. The Clintonville Farmers Market has a bike and stroller corral to encourage Saturday family outings, and the Pearl Market in downtown Columbus runs midday several times a week in-season, giving workers a reason to get out during their lunch hour. Visit Ohioproud.org for a full list of farmers markets around Columbus.

North Market Farmers Market
59 Spruce St., (614) 463-9664
northmarket.com

Clintonville Farmers Market
3519 N. High St.
in Clintonville
clintonvillefarmersmarket.org

Pearl Market
19 N. Pearl St.
(Pearl Alley, downtown)
downtowncolumbus.com

FARMERS MARKETS

Dublin Farmers Market
4261 W. Dublin Granville Rd. in Dublin
dublinfarmersmarket.com

Grandview Farmers Market
Grandview Ave. in Grandview
pearlalleygrowers.blogspot.com

Grove City Farmers Market
Grove City Town Center
gcchamber.org/farmers-market

Groveport Farmers Market
715 Main St. in Groveport
localharvest.org/groveport-farmers-market

Hilliard Farm Market
5445 Scioto Darby Rd. in Hilliard
hilliardfarmmarket.com

New Albany Farmers Market
202 E. Market St. in New Albany
newalbanyfarmersmarket.com

Olde Pickerington Farmers Market (year-round)
89 N. Center St. in Pickerington
pickeringtonvillage.com/farmers_market

Reynoldsburg Farmers Market
1520 Davidson Dr. in Reynoldsburg
ci.reynoldsburg.oh.us/departments/parks-and-recreation/farmers-market

Upper Arlington Farmers Market
1945 Ridgeview Rd. in Upper Arlington

Uptown Westerville Farmers Market
N. State St. and E. Home St. in Westerville
marketwednesday.com

Worthington Farmers Market
646 N. High St. in Worthington
worthingtonfarmersmarket.com

SIP COFFEE WITH PURPOSE
AT THE ROOSEVELT COFFEEHOUSE

Finally, there is a way to add more purpose to a cup of coffee beyond getting charged up for the day. The non-profit Roosevelt Coffeehouse uses proceeds from java sales to support more than a dozen agencies that fight hunger, human trafficking, and unclean water around the world. The coffeehouse even sources its beans directly from the farms of One Line Coffee and Stumptown Coffee Roasters, continuing its globally minded mission. Roosevelt Coffeehouse serves regular cups of Joe, espresso, V60 pour-over coffee, iced drinks, teas, and juices. To complete the experience (and feel even better about the purchase), try one of the creative Destination Donuts or a gluten-free pastry with your morning drink of choice.

The Roosevelt Coffeehouse
300 E. Long St., (614) 670-5228
rooseveltcoffee.org

TIP
The Roosevelt Coffeehouse is on the Columbus Coffee Trail powered by Experience Columbus. Sip your way through Columbus tasting the best coffee brews and earn points for a free Columbus Coffee T-shirt after visiting four or more locations. Find information at cbuscoffee.com.

TACKLE THE THURMANATOR CHALLENGE
AT THE THURMAN CAFÉ

No sandwich in Columbus has the reputation of the Thurmanator at The Thurman Café in German Village. Anyone who can finish the colossal burger in one sitting gets bragging rights and a new level of respect around town. Here's why: The Thurmanator is a twelve-ounce burger patty surrounded by a bun, mayo, lettuce, tomato, pickle, and banana peppers on the bottom and sautéed mushrooms and onions, ham, mozzarella & American cheese on top. It is served with French fries and a pickle spear. The Thurmanator challenge has gained even more popularity since being featured on the Travel Channel's *Man v. Food* television show. For those with smaller appetites, the restaurant serves an array of other burgers, hearty deli sandwiches, and Coney Island hot dogs with a secret homemade sauce served since The Thurman Café opened in Columbus in 1942.

The Thurman Café
183 Thurman Ave. in German Village, (614) 443-1570
thethurmancafe.com

STEP INTO A MODERN-DAY SPEAKEASY
AT THE LIGHT OF SEVEN MATCHSTICKS

The quiet and tucked-away Light of Seven Matchsticks lounge is a throwback to Prohibition-era Columbus. The hidden lounge is located below Natalie's Coal-Fired Pizza, which is a popular venue for live music acts. While the crowd gathers upstairs, the downstairs scene is another world with its dim lighting, velvet seating, and obscure and vintage cocktails. There is even a secret menu that patrons first have to find before they can order. Stepping inside the lounge means agreeing to speakeasy rules that include no cell phone service (to encourage dialogue) and respectful behavior while discussing sticky conversation topics like politics or religion. The adults-only establishment creates unforgettable craft cocktails like the "Running with Scissors and Playing with Matchsticks" concoction, which is a combination of brown buttered bourbon, Dolin dry vermouth, Benedictine, and house ancho syrup. Another to try is the "Cross Legged Snake," with fat-washed angostura, green Chartreuse, banana liqueur, lime, and pineapple.

The Light of Seven Matchsticks
5601 N. High St. in Worthington, (614) 436-2625
thelightofsevenmatchsticks.com

TRY A PANCAKE BALL
AT KATALINA'S

Foodies looking for a bit of vintage style to go along with a memorable meal should stop into Katalina's for a famous pancake ball and brunch. The small café is a renovated century-old gas station with a charming patio and a unique twist on traditional homemade food. Most people know Katalina's for the Original Pancake Balls™ that come in original or vegetarian options. Pancake balls use local stoneground flour and a filling that consists of Nutella, pumpkin-apple butter, dulce de leche, and maple syrup. The dish is served with thick-cut bacon for a near-overdose of the sweet and salty combo. Also try the breakfast tacos, Brussels sprouts hash, or avocado toast. The restaurant is only open for breakfast and lunch.

Katalina's
1105 Pennsylvania Ave., (614) 294-2233
katalinascafe.com

FIND OUT WHAT'S ON TAP
AT LOCAL BREWERIES

Columbus has a booming brew scene. The Brewery District near downtown Columbus is the original hub of breweries and still boasts many opportunities for an evening pub crawl, but many other locations are popping up with specialty brews and one-of-a-kind experiences. Try making a craft beer at North High Brewing using their equipment, sample experimental brews at the Land-Grant Brewing Company Taproom, or adopt-a-brew at Random Precision Brewing. True brew connoisseurs can tap into nearly a dozen growler shops that offer tastings, food, and special deals to fill up your beer growler. Columbus has more than fifty breweries to try. For an added incentive and a way to sample several breweries, hop on the Columbus Ale Trail that features more than forty-one breweries and offers prizes for stamps collected at each location. Research participating breweries and plot your route at cbusaletrail.com.

North High Brewing
1288 N. High St., (614) 407-5278
northhighbrewing.com

Random Precision Brewing
2365 W. Dublin-Granville Rd., (614) 389-3864
randomprecisionbrewing.com

Land-Grant Brewing Company
424 W. Town St. in Franklinton, (614) 427-3946
landgrantbrewing.com

Columbus Brewing Company
2555 Harrison Rd., (614) 224-3626
columbusbrewing.com

Elevator Brewery & Draught Haus
161 N. High St., (614) 228-0500
elevatorbrewing.com

Rockmill Tavern
503 S. Front St., (614) 732-4364
rockmilltavern.com

Hoof Hearted Brewery and Kitchen
850 N. Fourth St., (614) 401-4033
hoofheartedbrewing.com

BrewDog
96 Gender Rd. in Canal Winchester, (614) 908-3051
463 W. Town St. in Franklinton, (614) 908-3077
1175 N. High St. in the Short North, (614) 908-3053
brewdog.com

Wolf's Ridge Brewing
215 N. 4th St., (614) 429-3936
wolfsridgebrewing.com

Zaftig Brewing Company
7020A Huntley Rd. in Worthington, (614) 636-2537
drinkzaftig.com

CHOW DOWN
ON THE BEST HOT DOG IN COLUMBUS AT DIRTY FRANK'S

Go ahead, dream up the most extravagant hog dog imaginable. Chances are Dirty Frank's Hot Dog Palace serves it. This is where hot dog connoisseurs retreat to indulge in a taste that is as impressive as the extensive menu options. Bite into a bacon-wrapped dog with green chilies, refried beans, tomatoes, cheddar cheese, onions, and mayo or nosh on the "Picnic Table" dog served up with baked beans, cabbage and carrot mustard slaw, relish, and crushed potato chips. The options range from the plain "Birthday Suit" hot dog to the piled-on, piled-high, can't-fit-it-in-your-mouth dog. There are more than fifty a la carte toppings, including kimchi and pretzel bites. The eclectic menu, pop art, and atmosphere make Dirty Frank's an experience beyond just getting a full belly.

Dirty Frank's Hot Dog Palace
248 S. 4th St., (614) 824-4673
dirtyfrankscolumbus.com

TIP
Even vegans love Dirty Frank's. Most hot dogs come in vegetarian- or vegan-friendly versions and are easily identified on the menu.

DRESS UP
FOR DINNER

While Columbus is a casual city, it is still fun to dress to the nines and head out to dinner at some of the more refined dining establishments around town. Step into the quiet and classic Refectory Restaurant located inside a mid-1800s church that is now an elegant French restaurant. A Columbus mainstay since the 1980s, the Refectory has a notable and extensive wine list. Jeff Ruby's Steakhouse downtown has an elegant ambiance and a menu worthy of a special evening out. The U.S.D.A. Prime Steaks are hands-down some of the best in the city. Enjoy live entertainment as you savor fresh sushi, seafood and creative desserts. Jeff Ruby's has an extensive cocktail and wine list and even a cigar menu to commemorate those special occasions. M at Miranova is a classic modern dining experience with a refreshing view of the Columbus skyline accented with upscale decor. The cuisine is artistic American with European and Pacific Rim influences paired with a nationally recognized wine list making for an unforgettable evening on the town.

Refectory Restaurant
1092 Bethel Rd., (614) 451-9774
refectory.com

Jeff Ruby's Steakhouse
89 E. Nationwide Blvd.,
(614) 686-7800
jeffruby.com

M
2 Miranova Pl., Ste. 100
(614) 629-0000
matmiranova.com

EAT WITH CELEBRITIES
AT TOMMY'S DINER

Belly up to the counter at Tommy's Diner in Franklinton where the walls are covered with photos of celebrities who have stopped in for a bite. Slide into a red vinyl booth for a hearty breakfast or find a counter stool next to one of the regulars who is sipping coffee and ready to discuss the news of the day. It is common to see politicians and local news crews in Tommy's getting comments from customers on the latest headlines. The authentic diner has daily specials served up in large portions at small prices. No two visits at Tommy's Diner are ever the same. Owner Tommy Pappas changes out the photos on the walls regularly to showcase the local, national, and international celebrities who left behind autographed thank-you notes to Tommy over the years.

Tommy's Diner
914 W. Broad St., (614) 224-2422
tommysdiner.com

TIP
Columbus has several authentic diners around town where neon lights and made-to-order food are the norm, including Starliner Diner in Hilliard, Fitzy's Diner that is open twenty-four/seven, and George's Beechwold Diner in the Clintonville/Beechwold neighborhood.

SOCIALIZE
ON THE ROOFTOP AT JUNIPER

The only thing that can make a night out with friends even better is enjoying it on a rooftop patio in the fresh air with a perfect view of the Columbus skyline. The old Smith Brothers Hardware building in the heart of downtown features Juniper with the largest rooftop patio in the city. The upscale dining and craft cocktail venue provides panoramic views of downtown for those who are looking for a new kind of social scene. Juniper's craft gin cocktails feature locally distilled spirits with names that are reflective of local history and culture, like the "Park of Roses" and "Southside" drinks. The indoor-outdoor twelve-thousand-square-foot space is a popular spot for private events and easily one of best social settings in the city—and the one with the best view.

Juniper
580 N. 4th St., (614) 464-3333
juniperrooftop.com

TIP
Columbus has several smaller locations where socialites can enjoy rooftop libations, including Little Rock Bar and Seventh Son Brewing in Italian Village, the Crest Gastropub in Clintonville, BrewDog in Franklinton, Vaso in Dublin, and Novak's in downtown Columbus, which boasts one of the original rooftop patios.

LIFT YOUR SPIRITS
ON THE PATIO WITH A HAPPY HOUR

Socializing during Happy Hour is a *thing* in Columbus. Almost every restaurant and bar hosts a Happy Hour to satisfy every palate with small plates and small prices. A few stand out mostly because of their quaint patios, gossip-worthy drinks, or half-priced snacks that range from burgers and tacos to sushi and gourmet bites. Many locals like to end the workday at Lindey's in German Village, where the tree-shaded patio feels like a living room. Eleven at the Cap is an elegant wine bar with relaxing outdoor couches, five-dollar burgers, two-for-one small plates, and a front row seat to the always-interesting Short North people-watching extravaganza. Plan on staying awhile? Hit the Houlihan's Happy Hour in Upper Arlington with a five-dollar menu and "The Ridiculous Bloody Mary," a pitcher filled with Jose Cuervo Gold tequila, vodka, and Bloody Mary mix topped with a Thai glazed chicken wing, a stuffed 'shroom, and a slider.

Lindey's
169 E. Beck St. in German Village, (614) 228-4343
lindeys.com

Eleven
591 N. High St., (614) 225-9611
elevenatthecap.com

Houlihan's
3150 Tremont Rd. in Upper Arlington, (614) 326-2449
houlihans.com

Forno Kitchen + Bar
721 N. High St. in the Short North, (614) 469-0053
fornoshortnorth.com

Arch City Tavern
862 N. High St., (614) 725-5620
archcitytavern.com

Due Amici
67 E. Gay St., (614) 224-9373
due-amici.com

The 1126 Restaurant
1126 N. High St., (614) 725-3435
the1126columbus.com

Condado
1127 N. High St. in the Short North, (614) 928-3909
132 S. High St. in Downtown, (614) 456-7444
4077 Fenlon St. at Easton Town Center, (614) 532-5956
2977 N. High St. in Clintonville, (614) 230-2786
8958 Lyra Dr. at Polaris, (614) 896-8047
condadotacos.com

FIND YOUR ZEN WITH WINE AND YOGA
AT LOCAL ROOTS

Local Roots in Powell takes the farm-to-table concept to a whole new level with events that feed your state of mind along with your appetite. The restaurant philosophy is to serve simple and delicious food with a twist. In season, nearly ninety percent of the ingredients come from local sources, including some from the two-acre garden of owner Jessi Iams. The menu changes weekly depending on what is available from the small family farm that has a vegetable garden, a peach and apple orchard, chickens, and fourteen beehives. The rest of the menu features Ohio-sourced pork, all-natural Amish chicken, all-natural hormone-free beef, and Ohio bison. The "simple with a twist" philosophy extends beyond the food at Local Roots to the events at the restaurant like weekly wine and yoga classes, the paint and sip glassware workshops, and local artists playing live music on the patio.

Local Roots
15 E. Olentangy St. in Powell, (614) 602-8060
localrootspowell.com

TASTE A FRITTER
MADE FROM A SECRET FAMILY RECIPE

No one makes apple fritters like Grandma, and Columbus is fortunate to have a few bakeries that still make pastries from guarded-secret recipes brought to America by immigrants who settled in the city. Schneider's Bakery has churned out delicious donuts, coffee cakes, and birthday cakes from the same Westerville storefront for more than sixty-four years. Resch's Bakery was established by German immigrants more than a hundred years and six generations ago and still serves original recipe goodies like wedding cakes, rolls, holiday desserts, and fresh donuts. Every day, Auddino's Italian Bakery makes fresh bread for local restaurants and apple fritters that have a cult following. Also, not to be missed are the pastries, cookies, and Danish from the Original Goodie Shop in Upper Arlington that is still family-owned and still turning out delicious cookies after sixty years in the same location.

Schneider's Bakery
6 S. State St. in Westerville
(614) 882-6611
schneiders-bakery.com

Resch's Bakery
4061 E. Livingston Ave.
(614) 237-7421
reschbakery.com

Auddino's Italian Bakery
1490 Clara St., 614-294-2577

The Original Goodie Shop
2116 Tremont Center in Upper
Arlington, (614) 488-8777
theoriginalgoodieshop.com

LEARN
THE CRAFT DISTILLERY SCENE

Understanding the basics of the craft distillery scene in Columbus will get you a long way, or at least land you a unique cocktail around town. Columbus is home to two nationally recognized craft distillers: Middle West Spirits and Watershed Distillery. They are common names in Columbus because the distilleries are hometown favorites that made it big and still offer cool experiences for visitors. They also source the main ingredients used in the cocktails that are served at many local bars and restaurants. Middle West Spirits offers tours and tastings in their sixteen-thousand-square-foot facility that produces small batches of vodka, gin, and whiskey. Watershed Distillery creates gin, bourbon, apple brandy, and vodka and offers public tours twice a week. An easy way to learn some of the terminology is to visit the Watershed Kitchen & Bar, which lets patrons taste-test some of their creative cocktails. Drink flavors are enhanced by pairings with food inspired by the season.

Middle West Spirits
1230 Courtland Ave., (614) 299-2460
middlewestspirits.com

Watershed Distillery
1145 Chesapeake Ave., (614) 357-1936
watersheddistillery.com

GET KNEADY
AT FLOWERS & BREAD

It is hard to imagine how someone could dream up a culinary concept that combines bread making with flower arranging but the combo works for Flowers & Bread in Clintonville. The quaint café is a perfect place for coffee and a freshly made Danish, but its real charm is in the classes offered in the attached sunroom. Learn how to put on a wood-fired clam bake, create brunch dishes, finesse French cuisine, or bake fresh bread and summer tarts. Or learn the artistic technique of flower arranging with classes on spray roses, herbs and flowers, French bucket arrangements, and cake toppers. The cozy café highlights the simple things that bring pleasure as evidenced by its unpretentious name and the focus on two of life's most enjoyable things: bread and flowers.

Flowers & Bread
3870 N. High St. in Clintonville, (614) 262-5400
flowersandbread.com

TIP
Another local favorite that offers bread making and baking classes is Omega Artisan Baking in the North Market. Buy a loaf of fresh bread or learn how to make one on-site. Class information is at omegaartisanbakingoh.com.

MUSIC AND ENTERTAINMENT

CATCH A CONCERT

Columbus concert venues have stepped up their game attracting national and international musicians and artists from nearly every genre. Plan a night at Nationwide Arena, one of the top concert venues in the city when it is not hosting a Columbus Blue Jackets game. Nationwide Arena is in the heart of the Arena District surrounded by restaurants making it easy to grab a bite to eat before a concert. The Value City Arena in the Jerome Schottenstein Center is another top venue for evening concerts, drawing acts like Elton John, Smashing Pumpkins, and Journey. For a different type of concert experience, EXPRESS LIVE! is an indoor and outdoor venue in the Arena District and the first of its kind in the country, with an alternating backdrop depending on the artist and the season.

Nationwide Arena
200 W. Nationwide Blvd., (614) 246-2000
nationwidearena.com

The Jerome Schottenstein Center
555 Borror Dr., (614) 688-3939
schottensteincenter.com

EXPRESS LIVE!
405 Neil Ave., (614) 461-5483
promowestlive.com

PLACE YOUR BETS
AT HOLLYWOOD CASINO

Looking for the biggest poker room in Columbus? Hollywood Casino has it along with more than two thousand slot machines and seventy game tables. The Hollywood Casino is the only Vegas-style casino in Columbus. While gaming is the top draw for the Hollywood Casino, it is also an entertainment venue bringing in live music acts and evening entertainment featuring Ohio bands. The multiple large screens in the intimate H Lounge in the casino is a popular spot during noteworthy sporting events with spectators who come to watch the action unfold. There are several restaurants in the casino with a mix of food, from upscale dining at the steakhouse or a casual sandwich shop to a buffet that is popular on Friday nights for all-you-can-eat crab legs.

Hollywood Casino
200 Georgesville Rd., (614) 308-3333
hollywoodcolumbus.com

WATCH A CABARET PERFORMANCE
AT SHADOWBOX LIVE

Shadowbox Live in the Brewery District is Columbus's long-standing cabaret performance venue. Local performers present original works of sketch comedy in a cabaret-style club. What makes Shadowbox performances unique is that the actors are also the musicians, servers, and door greeters. It is hands-down one of the most enjoyable evenings of entertainment that you can find in Columbus. Shadowbox is the largest resident theatre company in the United States with a long history in the city. Take in one of the many shows—titles change on a regular basis—and be sure to see the traditional Holiday Hoopla show during November and December.

Shadowbox Live
503 S. Front St., Ste. 260, (614) 416-7625
shadowboxlive.org

TIP

The Short North Stage is another
place to take in a cabaret performance.
Its three venues—the Green Room, Ethel's
Lounge, and the recently renovated historic
Garden Theater—provide performance space
for the Columbus Moving Company, a
resident modern dance group.

Short North Stage
1187 N. High St., (614) 725-4042
shortnorthstage.org

GO APE
AT THE COLUMBUS ZOO & AQUARIUM

The Columbus Zoo & Aquarium is consistently ranked as one of the top zoos to visit in the United States. With six regions to explore and animals to observe like giraffes in Heart of Africa, elephants in Asia Quest, gorillas in the Congo Expedition, and manatees in the Aquarium, no two visits are the same. The zoo is focused on conservation and education, which is why there are regular close-encounter demonstrations and public animal feedings throughout the day for visitors to experience. There are even occasional zoo visits by Jungle Jack Hanna throughout the year. For the most personal, firsthand zoo experience, take part in one of the scheduled workshops or behind-the-scenes tours. Another special way to enjoy the Columbus Zoo is during a summer JazZoo concert, which is a musical evening and serenade at the Water's Edge Event Park with the Columbus Jazz Orchestra.

Columbus Zoo & Aquarium
4850 Powell Rd. in Powell, (614) 645-3550
columbuszoo.org

TIP
The annual Columbus Zoo Wildlights is an annual holiday tradition and a must-see experience with the zoo decorated in millions of LED lights, special exhibits, and a festive way to see the animals in the winter.

WATCH A BROADWAY SHOW
IN A RESTORED THEATRE

Broadway comes to Columbus throughout the year at the historic and stunningly restored Ohio and Palace Theatres. The Columbus Association for the Performing Arts (CAPA) brings in world-class Broadway performances and other entertainment acts, which regularly receive standing ovations from enthusiastic audiences. The restored 1928 Ohio Theatre provides Old World ambiance with its elegant Spanish-Baroque architecture, intricately painted ceilings, red crushed-velvet seating, and a masterful twenty-one-foot-high chandelier. In contrast, the Palace Theatre surrounds patrons with decorative French influences and a grand staircase entrance, a flashback to when the theatre was a vibrant vaudeville house in the 1930s, '40s, and '50s. The Southern Theatre, one of the oldest in the state opening in 1896, and the Lincoln Theatre, which was a symbolic venue for African American jazz influence, are restored theatres that also bring evening elegance and top live performing acts to Columbus.

Ohio Theatre
39 E. State St., (614) 469-0939
capa.com/venues/detail/ohio-theatre

Palace Theatre
34 W. Broad St., (614) 469-0939
capa.com/venues/detail/palace-theatre

Southern Theatre
21 E. Main St., (614) 469-0939
capa.com/venues/detail/southern-theatre

Lincoln Theatre
769 E. Long St., (614) 384-5640
lincolntheatrecolubus.com

GO TO THE COLUMBUS
ARTS FESTIVAL

The Columbus Arts Festival is one of the most anticipated and popular summer festivals in the capital city. The weekend-long festival takes place on the downtown riverfront and features juried artists from across the United States who sell paintings, sculptures, photography, leather, glass, wood carvings, and mixed-media artwork. Take a break from perusing the art by grabbing an overstuffed gyro or a scoop of ice cream from one of the local food truck vendors that line the riverfront streets. The festival is usually hot, so cool off under a shade tree by one of the performance stages on the festival grounds and enjoy live music, poetry, and dance demonstrations. The Columbus Arts Festival kicks off the summer season of fairs and celebrations of the many cultures and lifestyles that make up the city.

Columbus Arts Festival
columbusartsfestival.org

COLUMBUS FESTIVALS

Columbus Asian Festival
asian-festival.org

Columbus Greek Festival
columbusgreekfestival.com

Columbus International Festival
columbusinternationalfestival.org

Columbus Oktoberfest
columbusoktoberfest.com

Columbus PRIDE Festival
columbuspride.org

Comfest Community Festival
comfest.com

Creekside Blues & Jazz Festival in Gahanna
creeksidebluesandjazz.com

Dublin Irish Festival
dublinirishfestival.org

Festival Latino
festivallatino.net

Italian Festival
columbusitalianfestival.com

Jazz and Rib Festival
hotribscooljazz.org

Juneteenth Ohio Festival
juneteenthohio.net

WATCH LIVE HARNESS RACING
AT SCIOTO DOWNS

The edge-of-your-seat excitement of live harness racing has been available at Scioto Downs for Columbus racing enthusiasts since 1959. The seasonal sulky cart and trotter races take center stage from May through September on the outside track of what is now known as Eldorado Gaming Scioto Downs, making for an exciting afternoon or evening unlike any other entertainment in the city. Scioto Downs is also the place to watch simulcasting of top horse racing events like the Kentucky Derby, Belmont Stakes, and Preakness Stakes. Inside Eldorado Gaming Scioto Downs are video lottery terminals that were added in 2012 for additional gaming opportunities. There are regular lineups of live entertainment in addition to the racing and five restaurants on-site. The venue is open twenty-four hours a day, every day of the week, so there is always something to do at the Downs.

Scioto Downs
6000 S. High St., (614) 295-4700
sciotodowns.com

BREATHE DEEP
IN THE PARK OF ROSES

Stroll along the walking paths in the Park of Roses in Clintonville's Whetstone Park and soak in the fragrance of twelve thousand roses. There are more than four hundred rose varieties representing every hue and size imaginable. The thirteen-acre park is divided into sections: The Heritage Rose Garden features unique species that only bloom once a year; the Earth-Kind Rose Garden, with varieties grown using no fertilizers or pesticides; a Formal Rose Garden, with hybrid tea roses and modern varieties, and the Herb and Perennial gardens. The Park of Roses is a quiet retreat for reflection and a popular backdrop for weddings. As the largest rose garden park in the world owned by a city, it inspires peace and beauty with its memorial benches and fountains that enhance the experience of the breathtaking flowers.

Park of Roses
3901 N. High St. in Clintonville
parkofroses.org

TIP
The optimal time to visit the Park of Roses is during the full bloom from mid-June through mid-September. Sunday nights in the summer months are extra special at the park, with the Park of Roses Summer Concert Series featuring jazz and band performances at the gazebo.

PARK FOR A DOUBLE FEATURE
AT THE SOUTH DRIVE-IN THEATRE

Take a drive down memory lane to the South Drive-In Theatre for a nostalgic way to enjoy a double feature of first-run movies. The South Drive-In is one of the only old-school drive-in movie theatres left in Ohio. When you drive along the dirt road entrance, you will notice that not much has changed about the theatre from its heyday in the 1950s except for page-turns on the calendar. Every detail, from the unpaved driveway to the small concession stand serving only the movie basics of pop and popcorn, has been preserved and the audio still comes from metal speakers clipped onto the car windows. The South Drive-In opened in 1950 and has outlasted all of the drive-ins around Columbus that were popular during the subsequent decades. From April through September double-feature movies run on two outdoor screens, making it a wholesome night out for the entire family.

South Drive-In Theatre
3050 S. High St., (614) 491-6771
drive-inmovies.com

TIP

Show up early to the South Drive-In and bring your portable grill for a tailgate cookout before the show. Grills must be out before the movie starts but you can nosh on your burgers and bratwurst during showtime.

PLAN
A GALLERY HOP

At least once while you are in Columbus it is essential for you to experience an evening of art appreciation at a Short North Gallery Hop. The Short North Arts District comes alive on Hop nights as musicians and artists entertain passers-by on the sidewalks while the galleries in the District stay open late to showcase original local and international art pieces for viewing or for purchase. The monthly Gallery Hop is one of the best local culture scenes in the city. Start with a drink or dinner at a lively restaurant or bar along High Street, like Arch City Tavern, Lemongrass, Marcella's, Happy Greek, or Hyde Park Prime Steakhouse located on the Cap that connects the Short North to Downtown. Then spend the evening strolling through the galleries and shops that feature local goods, international imports that support charities, and new artist exhibits. After the galleries close, stick around for the nightlife that gets even more vibrant after 10 p.m. at the karaoke and dance clubs.

Short North Arts District
shortnorth.org

TIP

The Holiday Hop in December is a festive way to enjoy one of these Gallery nights. The storefronts and district streets are decked out in holiday themes, and the restaurants and bars pour out their best sips to warm you from the inside out with concoctions like spiked apple cider and gourmet hot cocoa while you search for the perfect gift to enhance a loved one's art collection (or yours).

BUILD SOMETHING
AT LEGOLAND® DISCOVERY CENTER

There is nothing else in Columbus quite like the LEGOLAND® Discovery Center at Easton Town Center. It is a LEGO fanatic's dream come true. There are several LEGO® building zones where creativity can go wild and a behind-the-scenes LEGO® factory tour showing how the timeless plastic building pieces are made in so many shapes, sizes, and colors. Slide on a pair of goggles to experience the 4D cinema, where 3D LEGO® films are combined with wind, rain, and snow in the theater to make you a part of the action on the screen. Or pick up a few building tips from a master LEGO® builder in the creative workshop. There are rides, play zones for kids, and interactive games for the entire family. Be sure to check out Miniland, which features small-scale LEGO® structures of Columbus, Cincinnati, and Cleveland made out of 1.5 million tiny LEGO® pieces.

LEGOLAND® Discovery Center
165 Easton Town Center, (614) 407-7721
columbus.legolanddiscoverycenter.com

SPEND AN EVENING
WITH THE SYMPHONY

The highlight of summer evenings at the Columbus Commons is the Picnic with the Pops series of performances by the Columbus Symphony Orchestra. Pack up a chair or blanket and a picnic to enjoy a symphony under the stars in Columbus's most popular green space. Various entertainers like pop singer Rick Springfield or the OSU marching band join the Columbus Symphony Orchestra for unique performances. The genres range from jazz and classic rock to hip hop. Table seating is available, and the food vendors on-site make it easy to relax for the evening if you don't want to carry all your gear. A special series for families and kids ages three to twelve called the Popcorn Pops introduces youngsters to the joy of live symphony entertainment, allowing them to dance to kid-themed music.

Picnic with the Pops
Summers at the Columbus Commons, (614) 228-9600
columbussymphony.com

CELEBRATE
INDEPENDENT FILMS

Columbus is a creative city that celebrates independent films in a big way. The Drexel Theatre in Bexley is a favorite for indie film lovers for its quaint theater experience and unique independent and international films. Look for Drexel events throughout the year, including the America's Greatest Films series that capitalizes on fan favorites like *American Graffiti* and *Dr. Strangelove* or the popular Sci-Fi marathons. The Gateway Film Center is a hub for independent movies, with a different lineup every week. It offers events for like-minded independent movie fans to gather, discuss, and enjoy new flicks together. A few other historic movie houses that make for a unique cinematic experience in central Ohio include the Studio 35 Cinema & Drafthouse in Clintonville, the oldest independent theater in the city, and the Grandview Theater & Drafthouse, a charmingly renovated 1926 theater with a single movie screen.

TIP
Indie movie fans should check out the annual Columbus International Film & Animation Festival put on by Columbus College of Art & Design (CCAD) featuring globally acclaimed independent films and the oldest film festival in the United States.

Drexel Theatre
2254 E. Main St. in Bexley, (614) 231-9958
drexel.net

Gateway Film Center
1550 N. High St., (614) 247-4433
gatewayfilmcenter.org

Studio 35 Cinema & Drafthouse
3055 Indianola Ave. in Clintonville, (614) 261-1581
studio35.com

Grandview Theater & Drafthouse
1247 Grandview Ave. in Grandview, (614) 670-4102
grandviewtheater.com

Columbus Film Festival
columbusfilmfestival.org

MARVEL AT THE BUTTER SCULPTURE
AT THE OHIO STATE FAIR

Ohio's dairy roots take center stage during the grand unveiling of the butter cow sculpture each year at the Ohio State Fair. If you are going to the fair, this experience is a must. The butter sculpture is actually an entire themed scene behind the refrigerated glass in the Dairy Barn that is a guarded secret until the first day of the fair each year. The tradition goes back to the early 1900s and honors Ohio's dairy history and the 2,200 dairy farms that still exist in the state. The first butter sculpture in 1903 appropriately featured a cow and a calf. Every year since then, the themes and displays have become more elaborate. Themes have ranged from a tribute to the Ohio State Buckeye football team to Darth Vader, from the Monopoly board game to outer space featuring Ohio native John Glenn. Take some time to marvel at the craftsmanship carved out of hundreds of pounds of butter, then get an ice cream cone made with Ohio-fresh dairy products in the fair's Dairy Barn.

Ohio State Fair
717 E. 17th Ave.
ohiostatefair.com

PLAY
AT THE COLUMBUS COMMONS

Spend a day at a festival, an evening at an outdoor concert, a Saturday doing yoga in the park, or a lunch hour watching families on the carousel at the Columbus Commons. Located on the site of the old City Center Mall, which holds many downtown memories for locals, the repurposed land is now a community gathering spot and green space. There are family and kid-specific events on the calendar like Family Fun Day and Movie Nights featuring outdoor flicks on giant screens. The Columbus Commons hosts festivals and social events throughout the year, including regular outdoor concerts and free fitness classes like Zumba, yoga, and aerobics on the lawn, giving locals plenty of opportunities to get out for some fresh air. It is also a perfect spot to sit and enjoy a cup of coffee on a bench in the center of downtown.

Columbus Commons
160 S. High St., (614) 603-2560
columbuscommons.org

CELEBRATE
WITH THE CITY
DOWNTOWN

Holidays are taken pretty seriously around Columbus especially when they provide a good excuse to bring the family out to celebrate. There are several opportunities to join a few hundred thousand friends in the heart of downtown during the year: Red, White & Boom! Independence Day Celebrations in July, HighBall Halloween in October, and the First Night Columbus New Year's Eve celebration in December.

Ooh and aah at the largest fireworks demonstration in the state at Red, White & Boom! It is an annual tradition for more than half-a-million Columbusites to celebrate Independence Day. It takes place July 3 in downtown Columbus with entertainment, parades, food, family games, a sea of people, and of course the main fireworks event at dusk over the downtown skyline. Deck yourself out in costume in October for the city's fundraising celebration of HighBall Halloween. It is part fashion runway and part masquerade as thirty thousand people fill the Short North streets. The costumed revelers make for an exciting visual spectacle at the two-day combination street party, local bands concert, and costume party. Ring in the New Year with First Night Columbus, the annual family-friendly celebration with evening activities at COSI, musical entertainment, and a New Year's countdown at midnight.

Red, White & Boom!
July 3, Downtown
redwhiteandboom.org

HighBall Halloween
Last weekend in October, Short North District
highballcolumbus.org

First Night Columbus
December 31, Downtown
firstnightcolumbus.com

CATCH
THE NEXT BIG BAND

The local music scene in Columbus thrives in venues from the intimate lounge environment of Natalie's Coal-Fired Pizza and Live Music to the notorious Newport Music Hall, which has featured local and national acts like B.B. King, Red Hot Chili Peppers, Pearl Jam, and Anthrax. Lots of local acts cut their teeth in the music industry in small Columbus venues. PromoWest has a number of venues in proximity to one another that support the emerging music scene. The A&R Music Bar is known for grooming up-and-coming performers who eventually go on to become popular mainstream acts, including Fall Out Boy and O.A.R. The Basement, located beneath A&R Music Bar, gives emerging musicians a supportive place to perform and to grow their grassroots following of fans. Columbus has live music venues to suit every mood and niche, from low-key jazz to hard-core heavy metal.

LIVE MUSIC VENUES

Natalie's Coal-Fired Pizza and Live Music
5601 N. High St. in Worthington, (614) 436-2625
nataliescoalfiredpizza.com

Newport Music Hall
1722 N. High St., (614) 461-5483
promowestlive.com

Ace of Cups
2619 N. High St., (614) 262-6001
aceofcupsbar.com

A&R Music Bar
The Basement
391 Neil Ave., (614) 461-5483
promowestlive.com

Rumba Café
2507 Summit St., (614) 268-1841
columbusrumbacafe.com

Skully's Music-Diner
1151 N. High St., (614) 291-8856
skullys.org

Dick's Den
2417 N. High St., (614) 268-9573
dicksdencolumbus.com

Woodlands Tavern
1200 W. 3rd Ave. in Grandview, (614) 299-4987
woodlandstavern.com

Big Room Bar
1036 S. Front St., (614) 449-9612
bigroombar.com

The Spacebar
2590 N. High St. in Clintonville
spacebarcolumbus.com

The Tree Bar
919 McMillen Ave., (614) 725-0955
treebarcolumbus.com

EXPLORE NEW IDEAS
AT THE IDEA FOUNDRY

Want to start a small business or take crafting to a new level? The Idea Foundry in Columbus is filled with inspiration and the tools to turn great artistic ideas into reality. The Idea Foundry is located inside a century-old renovated shoe factory with more than twenty thousand square feet of workshop space, a tool shop, and assembly areas for large projects. Take a class to learn how to make a mini baseball bat, assemble a stained-glass window hanging, or blacksmith your own knife out of a railroad stake. The Idea Foundry hosts workshops, speakers, and events to get the creative juices flowing and to give the artistic community in Columbus plenty of ways to express themselves. The Idea Foundry also offers tours for those who want to check things out first and see crafters bringing their ideas to life before committing to a project of their own.

The Idea Foundry
421 W. State St., (614) 653-8068
ideafoundry.com

PUCKER UP AND BLOW
AT THE AMERICAN WHISTLE CORPORATION

No one can resist blowing a whistle, but most people do not know that the small noise-maker and potential life-saver is made in Columbus at the American Whistle Corporation. It is the only manufacturer of metal whistles in the United States. Take a forty-five-minute tour through the factory to learn all the little secrets about making whistles like how the tiny ball gets inside and what materials are used to make them so reliable. You will also get a peek at the modern and antique machinery that has been and is now used to make the whistles. While touring the plant, learn about the programs for keeping communities safe, like the Whistle Defense Program promoted by the American Whistle Corporation for use by companies, universities, and law enforcement. Visitors to the factory may never look at whistles the same way again.

American Whistle Corporation
6540 Huntley Rd., (614) 846-2918
americanwhistle.com

Credit: Columbus Blue Jackets

SPORTS AND RECREATION

SCORE A WIN
AT A COLUMBUS CLIPPERS
BASEBALL GAME

Spending a night out at Huntington Park to watch a Columbus Clippers baseball game is a time-honored tradition in Columbus. The Columbus Clippers, a Triple-A affiliate of the Cleveland Indians Major League Baseball team, fires up home runs beneath the city skyline during seasonal home games in the Arena District. Take a stroll along the main deck for dinner options ranging from BBQ pork and grilled chicken to the traditional ballgame hot dog. Enjoy a cocktail on the rooftop terrace or grab some take-out on the way and toss a blanket in the picnic area before the game. Most Clippers games have special promotions or giveaways and the famous mascot race featuring Lou Seal. Join local fans to cheer on the hometown team during an afternoon or evening under the stadium lights, capped off with fireworks.

Huntington Park
330 Huntington Park Ln. in the Arena District, (614) 462-5250
huntingtonparkcolumbus.com

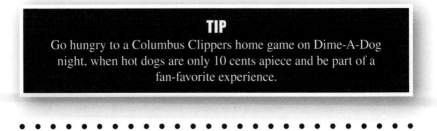

TIP
Go hungry to a Columbus Clippers home game on Dime-A-Dog night, when hot dogs are only 10 cents apiece and be part of a fan-favorite experience.

KAYAK
ON THE SCIOTO RIVER

The Scioto Riverfront in downtown Columbus is the centerpiece of the city. On weekend afternoons from May through October, colorful kayaks dot the river adding an exciting recreational activity to the downtown landscape. The Paddle in the City program run by HERO U.S.A. gives city-dwellers a chance to relax and enjoy a bit of nature in the middle of the towering downtown development. For three seasons of the year nature lovers can rent kayaks and paddle along the Scioto River while festivals and entertainment events take place alongside the waterfront. Those new to kayaking and paddle boarding can take an introductory lesson and a 3.6-mile guided trip along the river. The certified instructors teach paddle techniques and kayaking skills while providing nature education about the area. So, grab your paddle and enjoy a unique perspective of Columbus from the water.

Paddle in the City
650 W. Nationwide Blvd.
paddleinthecity.com

SHOUT OUT O-H-I-O
AT AN OHIO STATE BUCKEYE FOOTBALL GAME

Game day Saturdays in Columbus are sacred. Ohio State University Buckeye Football fans are either at the Ohio Stadium (nicknamed the Shoe, short for Horseshoe) or flocking to local bars and restaurants with big screens to capture every Buckeye touchdown. Taking in an actual game should be on everyone's must-do list in Columbus but no matter how fans support the team, wearing scarlet and grey and offering a spontaneous shout of "O-H" and responding to the chant with an "I-O" around town is all part of the tradition. Fans know that the actual football game is only part of the game day experience. Buckeye football tailgating is a favorite pastime in the city and joining in the revelry is easy. The parking lots around the stadium are ground-zero for tailgate parties that kick off in the early morning hours on home game days.

Ohio State Buckeyes
ohiostatebuckeyes.com

HIT THE TRAIL
IN A METRO PARK

The metropolitan side of Columbus is thriving but every now and then it is nice to take a quiet stroll in one of Columbus's nineteen Metro Parks. The Metro Parks are scattered throughout the city serving as small retreats where cosmopolitans and suburbanites can find respite in nature. Try rock climbing at Scioto Audubon Park, get out on the water and canoe at Prairie Oaks, look for eagles nesting at Highbanks Metro Park, or watch bison roam in Battelle Darby Creek Park. All of the parks have regular nature programs, from full moon hikes and searching for salamanders to kids' fishing clinics and stargazing. All of the parks feature relaxing ways to unwind with open fields for games of Frisbee, picnics, and activities like birding or archery.

Metro Parks
metroparks.net

TIP
Get Fido outdoors to enjoy nature on one of the designated pet trails featured at nearly all of the Metro Parks. Some of the parks even offer fenced-in dog run areas and designated dog swimming areas.

CHEER ON
THE COLUMBUS BLUE JACKETS

The Columbus Blue Jackets know how to fire up a crowd! Jump into the fray from September through April at Nationwide Arena when Columbus's National Hockey League Team takes to the ice, driving the puck and scoring points. Since their inaugural 2000-01 season, the Blue Jackets, a name that pays homage to Ohio's contributions to American history during the Civil War, have consistently ranked tops in the NHL for the fan experience. A game highlight is the firing of the 1857 replica Napoleon field cannon each time the home team scores a goal. Another favorite CBJ game tradition happens during the national anthem when the audience is directed to turn their attention to fellow fan and classically trained opera singer Leo Welsh. Before the opening note the crowd erupts with a loud greeting of "LEO!"

Nationwide Arena
200 W. Nationwide Blvd. in the Arena District
nhl.com/bluejackets

TIP
Arrive early at Nationwide Arena to catch the pregame warmup skate for the half hour before puck drop. Watch the team practice from ice level and maybe even catch a puck that soars over the glass.

ZIP LINE
IN THE MOONLIGHT

ZipZone Outdoor Adventures gives adrenaline junkies a whole different reason to anticipate a full moon. The guided moonlight zip line tours take place every month during the full moon allowing the adventurous to zoom through the treetops in the dark. The outdoor adventure park is just north of Columbus at Camp Mary Orton, where those needing a break from the norm can take several types of zip line tours or embark on a high ropes adventure. Even kids can get in on the action with programs designed specifically for adventurers-in-training. The ZipZone Outdoor Adventures company focuses on conservation and environmental protection, so all of the zip line courses are constructed to be environmentally friendly. The courses are designed to expose participants to the old-growth trees in the park without destroying some of Columbus's most prime natural environment.

ZipZone Outdoor Adventures
7925 N. High St., (614) 847-9477
zipzonetours.com

SEE THE CITY ON TWO WHEELS
WITH SEGAWAY TOURS

One of the most unique ways to explore the lay of the land in Columbus is with a Segway tour. SegAway Tours take riders past some of the most iconic and important landmarks in Columbus, including the courthouse, Ohio Statehouse, and the North Market. Seeing some of the best parts of downtown on two wheels from March through December is an active way to experience the highlights of the city while spending some time outdoors. The Original City Tour covers the top historical and culturally significant spots in Columbus while the River & Bridges Tour wheels riders over the newer bridges in the downtown area where they can get a glimpse of bikers and kayakers enjoying the Scioto Mile. This tour also lets you experience the bridges' unique architecture along with the statues and sculptural pieces that adorn them and add character and ambiance to the downtown skyline.

SegAway Tours
400 N. High St. inside the Greater Columbus Convention Center
(614) 222-3005
segawaytoursofcolumbus.com

SPORT BLACK & GOLD
FOR THE COLUMBUS CREW SC

If you see an abundance of black and gold apparel around town, it is because the Columbus Crew SC, the city's Major League Soccer team, has an allegiant fan base. Soccer fanatics break out the black and gold during season games and sport other merchandise throughout the year, rivaling the scarlet and gray worn in support of the Ohio State Buckeyes. The casual fans can show support for the Crew with game tickets and wearing team colors. The hardcore soccer fans can join the Hudson Street Hooligans, a devoted Crew fan club that typically occupies a section of the stadium on game days. The Crew came to Columbus in 1994 as one of the ten inaugural MLS teams. Its fan base started strong but solidified after winning the 2008 MLS Cup championship.

columbuscrewsc.com
hudsonstreethooligans.com

TACKLE
A CORN MAZE

Ohio has proud agricultural roots, so the fall season means sweet corn and corn mazes at local farms on the fringes of the city. Lynd Fruit Farm in Pataskala is famous for themed corn mazes with trails in the shapes of superheroes and iconic movies like *The Wizard of Oz*. Your mission in the eight-acre maze is to follow a series of clues and trails that eventually lead to an exit. Circle S Farms in Grove City celebrates all things fun in the fall with corn and sunflower mazes, and Dill's Greenhouse in Groveport has a five-acre corn maze. Navigating a corn maze is harder than it sounds, but fear not; there's always an emergency exit strategy for those who get lost.

Lynd Fruit Farm
9393 Morse Rd. in Pataskala, (740) 927-8559
lyndfruitfarm.com

Circle S Farms
9015 London Groveport Rd. in Grove City, (614) 878-7980
circlesfarm.com

Dill's Greenhouse
5800 Rager Rd. in Groveport, (614) 836-3700

TIP

Plan a whole day around a corn maze visit, as the farms that offer them also have orchards where you can pick baskets of fresh fruit and opportunities to participate in other activities like fall festivals, hayrides, and you-pick pumpkin patches.

PICNIC
IN AN IMPRESSIONIST PAINTING AT THE TOPIARY PARK

The Topiary Park in Columbus is a treasure that is tucked away behind the Columbus Metropolitan Library on the site of the former Ohio School for the Deaf. An entire section of the park portrays a life-size topiary interpretation of the famous painting by post-Impressionist painter George Seurat, *A Sunday Afternoon on the Island of La Grande Jatte.* Walk around the topiary figures to admire the horticulture and artistic detail, then step back across the lawn to soak in how the fifty-four manicured sculptures create a stunning life-size display of the famous painting. The setting is perfect for a picnic lunch, especially in mid-summer when the topiary figures on the grounds and in the boats on the water are at their best.

The Topiary Park
40 E. Town St., (614) 645-0197
topiarypark.org

TIP
Stop by the Gatehouse & Visitors Center on the south side of the park to pick up unique gifts and to support the continued upkeep of the topiary park. For a more in-depth visit you can schedule a docent-led tour by contacting the Friends of the Topiary Park through the Park's website.

PAY HOMAGE
TO THE GOLDEN BEAR

One of the most beloved sports figures in Columbus is golfing
legend Jack Nicklaus, so it is no surprise that the Jack Nicklaus
Museum features one of the most impressive collections of golf
memorabilia and a fascinating timeline of the life of the Golden Bear
himself. It is fitting that the museum has more than two thousand
pieces in the collection honoring Columbus's hometown hero and
the game that Nicklaus has influenced so much. The galleries give
visitors insight into Nicklaus's personal history, his contributions
to golf, and the highlights of a sports career that includes more
than one hundred professional wins. Stop into the Nicklaus Family
Room to get a glimpse of his family life from childhood and see
his career highlights. The Memorial Tournament Gallery features
artifacts and educational pieces about the prestigious annual local
tournament on the PGA tour.

Jack Nicklaus Museum
2355 Olentangy River Rd., (614) 247-5959
nicklausmuseum.org

FEEL A CHILL YEAR-ROUND
AT THE CHILLER ICE RINK

It might be hard to believe that people in Columbus actually seek out the chill of the ice after the long Ohio winter season comes to an end, but the Chiller ice rink gives people a reason to enjoy the cold all year long. The Chiller rink has four locations in the city, with public skating times and lessons. Stop into the rinks at Easton, Dublin, Lewis Center, or the Arena District to give ice skating a go and to have something fun to do with the family even in the middle of summer. All of the rinks have events throughout the year, like the Friday Night Meltdown for teenagers and drop-in skating times. Those who get the ice itch more frequently can take figure skating or speed skating lessons or sign up for an ice hockey class to up their skills.

OhioHealth Chiller Easton
3600 Chiller Ln. near Easton Town
Center, (614) 475-7575
thechiller.com

OhioHealth Chiller North
8144 Highfield Dr. in Lewis Center
(740) 549-0009
thechiller.com

OhioHealth Chiller Dublin
7001 Dublin Park Dr. in Dublin
(614) 764-1000
thechiller.com

OhioHealth Ice Haus
200 W. Nationwide Blvd. in the
Arena District, (614) 246-3380
thechiller.com

BIKE THROUGH TOWN ON A WHIM
WITH COGO BIKE SHARE

When the mood strikes to bicycle through Columbus, it is easy grab a set of wheels from one of the many CoGo Bike Share stations in downtown and go. Columbus is a bike-friendly city with dedicated bicycle lanes and forty-six CoGo Bike rental stations around the downtown area. Rent bikes with a day pass or get a membership. Plenty of downtown workers save the hassle of parking a car by using the bikes to get to meetings and lunch during business hours. There are bike stations close to the Scioto Mile and North Bank Park, which are connected by a bike trail along the downtown riverfront. For longer excursions, hop onto the Scioto Trail, Alum Creek Trail, Olentangy Trail, or one of the many bike trails that stretch beyond downtown and into city suburbs that are all connected in an extensive network.

CoGo Bike Share
Stations throughout downtown, (855) 877-2646
cogobikeshare.com

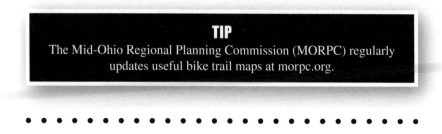

TIP
The Mid-Ohio Regional Planning Commission (MORPC) regularly
updates useful bike trail maps at morpc.org.

FISH
IN A PUBLIC POND

Tucked away within the urban growth of Columbus is a cluster of small public ponds into which kids, families, and avid anglers can throw a line to fish for bass, trout, bluegill, and catfish. Several ponds in Franklin County, like Heritage Park and Antrim Park, are stocked with rainbow trout by the Ohio Department of Natural Resources to encourage fishing. There is fishing allowed in ponds at ten Metro Parks around town. The ponds at Chestnut Ridge, Sharon Woods, and Slate Run are designated for kids ages fifteen and younger only. Anglers who enjoy stream fishing can do that at Highbanks, Scioto Audubon Metro Park, Big and Little Darby Creeks, Scioto Grove Metro Park, and at various public locations on the Scioto River. Dublin is one of several suburbs that stocks the city's ponds in its parks with various fish species. A favorite is the pond at the M.L. Red Trabue Nature Reserve.

Local Fishing Resources
ohiodnr.gov
metroparks.net
dublinohiousa.gov

TIP
Be sure to obtain a valid fishing license from the Ohio Department of Natural Resources Division of Wildlife and read state and community fishing regulations before casting for that picture-worthy catch.

GET PUMPED
AT THE ARNOLD CLASSIC

Sports and fitness fanatics can get their pump on at the annual Arnold Schwarzenegger Sports Festival and can continue to celebrate the fitness icon throughout the year. Arnold is fond of Columbus and people in the city are fond of him as evidenced by the statue depicting his likeness outside of the Columbus Convention Center. The annual Arnold Sports Festival draws more than eighteen thousand bodybuilding and fitness competitors each spring—usually in March—and thousands more spectators. The competition and fitness expo is open to the public and features more than seventy disciplines that range from powerlifting and wrestling to martial arts and dance. Schwarzenegger makes regular appearances at the festival and occasionally visits Columbus throughout the year, so an Arnold sighting is likely in Cbus.

Arnold Sports Festival
Greater Columbus Convention Center
400 N. High St.
arnoldsportsfestival.com

GET IN YOUR STEPS
ALONG THE SCIOTO MILE

It is easy to log those ten thousand steps a day by taking a lunch break or after-work jog on the Scioto Mile along the downtown riverfront. The paved multi-use path is a quiet natural retreat in the shadow of the downtown skyline. The Scioto Mile stretches from the Arena District to the Whittier Peninsula and is lined with park benches, swing sets, and fountains. Run, walk, bike, or just relax in the 175-acre green space and park setting along the Scioto River. One of the best views of the Scioto Mile can be had from the Milestone 229 restaurant located on the waterfront. Stop in for lunch or an evening cocktail with a perfect sunset view from the windows overlooking Bicentennial Park.

Scioto Mile
Along the downtown riverfront
sciotomile.com

Milestone 229
229 Civic Center Dr., (614) 427-0276
milestone229.com

MEET
BRUTUS BUCKEYE

The pride of the Ohio State Buckeyes is mascot Brutus Buckeye, who struts his stuff and engages fans during OSU sporting events. While meeting Brutus in person at an event is photo-worthy, so is a selfie with one of his statue namesakes located around campus. The artistically themed fiberglass Brutus statues were created for a fundraiser called "Brutus on Parade" for the William Oxley Thompson Memorial Library renovation in 2007. There were fifty statues during the campaign and while some of them were sold, there are still about thirty-four scattered around the campus area. They are easy to spot. Standing on two-thousand-pound concrete bases, the Brutus statues are each six foot two inches tall and weigh 150 pounds. Each Brutus has a theme, like the *Rock N' Roll Brutus* located at the Schottenstein Center, or the *Woody Hayes Brutus* at the Ohio Union, or *First Buckeye in Space Brutus* at Page Hall.

TIP
A group called Ohio Staters keeps tabs on the Brutus statue locations and publishes a map of all known public locations on their website at u.osu.edu/ohiostaters.

GROW A GREEN THUMB
IN A COMMUNITY GARDEN

Columbus is community minded all the way down to its roots, literally, as evidenced by the small neighborhood gardens located throughout the city. While individual neighborhoods maintain their rules for participation and cultivation in community garden plots, the City of Columbus is using the concept to beautify vacant properties around town. There are ninety-five parcels available to license as part of the City of Columbus Land Bank Community Garden Program. New parcels cost $50 and $10 for renewals and garden plots come with water tanks, compost, and soil for gardeners. Anyone can apply, so get a set of gardening tools and start digging in the dirt. The biggest challenge will be choosing what flowers and vegetables to plant.

Columbus Community Garden Program
(614) 645-5263
columbus.gov/landredevelopment/communitygardens

TIP
Need gardening tools? The Rebuilding Together Central Ohio organization has a tool library with thousands of tools available for loan at rtcentralohio.org, and the Franklin Park Conservatory offers classes and resources for community gardeners through its Growing to Green Program at fpconservatory.org.

CULTURE AND HISTORY

GET CHARGED
BY AN ELECTROSTATIC GENERATOR
AT COSI

While the experience sounds scarier than it is, the hair-raising electrostatic generator at the Center of Science and Industry (COSI) is one of the classics. COSI remains an original must-do entertainment venue in Columbus, and it is the centerpiece of the downtown riverfront. COSI makes learning about science fun with live shows and hundreds of hands-on exhibits, from the Big Science Park, where kids can lift a 2,437-pound car, to an ocean research area where they can climb into a mini-submarine. Seek out the American Museum of Natural History Dinosaur Gallery to watch a model Tyrannosaurus rex walk and learn how paleontologists use this type of replication in their research of this species. Test the science of balance and gravity by hopping on the High Wire Unicycle located two stories above the ground and hold steady while riding across the eighty-four-foot cable. Round out a day at COSI in its planetarium, the largest in Ohio, and explore the galaxy beneath its sixty-foot dome while watching their state-of-the-art projection show.

COSI
333 W. Broad St., (614) 228-2674
cosi.org

CHANNEL YOUR INNER AUTHOR
AT THE THURBER HOUSE

Connoisseurs of literature find respite at the Thurber House, which is the restored home of author and cartoonist James Thurber. Walk the narrow hallways to see where Thurber spent many of his years collecting inspiration for his literary collections. Be sure to visit his second-floor bedroom and office and the museum collection of Thurber memorabilia. The Thurber House hosts programs throughout the year celebrating literature with writing classes, workshops, and author readings. Two of the notable programs are the Evenings with Authors and the Summer Literary Picnics in which authors are invited to showcase recent works. The summer event features Ohio authors and takes place outside on the lawn with picnic dinners against the backdrop of Thurber's home. The Thurber House is on the National Register of Historic Places and is a must-visit for anyone who has an affection for acerbic wit and humorous literature.

Thurber House
77 Jefferson Ave., (614) 464-1032
thurberhouse.org

TRY GHOST HUNTING
AT THE STATEHOUSE

The Ohio Statehouse and its grounds is a great place to visit any time of the year, but a fun way to explore this stunning piece of state history is during the seasonal Haunted Statehouse Tours in the fall. While the tours are family-friendly, they focus on points of interest at the statehouse with stories and information that include alleged paranormal activity that has been reported along the building's limestone corridors. Listen to accounts of sightings of Abraham Lincoln's ghost, which reportedly roams the hallways of the Capitol building. Find out about the spirits of Civil War–era soldiers that are rumored to have been spotted in the statehouse since their deaths when the building was used as a hospital for the critically wounded. Tours are led by volunteers dressed in character taking the curious through statehouse passageways by lantern light.

Ohio Statehouse
1 Capitol Square, (614) 752-9777
ohiostatehouse.org

TIP

Tickets for the tours go fast when they start selling in early fall. So plan ahead. Arrive early for the tour to enjoy activities that include the option to write a message in a Ghost Post to one of the resident spirits.

PLAY VINTAGE LAWN GAMES
AT THE OHIO VILLAGE

While it is not common to see people trying their skills on stilts around Columbus, the one place where vintage lawn games like hop and stick are the norm is at the Ohio History Connection's Ohio Village. The village is an outdoor living museum with period actors and a town replicated to exactly the way it was in 1890. Give a speech on the steps of the Town Hall with scripts that model mid-nineteenth-century language or dress up in vintage costumes for an old-fashioned photo. A visit is not complete without going into the Ohio History Center next to the Ohio Village. Stroll through interactive exhibits that showcase battle flags, unearthed Ohio relics, and life in the Heartland throughout the decades with a look at what ideas and inventions were dominating society in pop culture, politics, and industry at various periods in Ohio history.

Ohio History Center
800 E. 17th Ave., (614) 297-2300
ohiohistory.org

TIP

Plan a visit when the Ohio Village Muffins have a baseball game. It is a treat to see reenactors sliding into home base in vintage baseball gear and playing by the original ballgame rules.

FIND A NEW WAY TO HONOR VETERANS
AT THE NATIONAL VETERANS MEMORIAL AND MUSEUM

Columbus is home to the National Veterans Memorial and Museum (NVMM), which provides visitors with unique personal perspectives of American war veterans. Through multimedia experiences, personal letters, photos, and interactive exhibits, visitors go on a journey to the front lines of combat through the private and harrowing insight of war veterans and their families. Take a walk through the elm trees in the elegantly landscaped Memorial Grove and stroll out on the grounds to find historical and symbolic representation in the details of the architecture and landscaping. Find reflective solitude on the rooftop sanctuary to honor the selfless service and sacrifice of military men and women around the country and throughout American history. The permanent and temporary exhibits are designed to take visitors on an immersive experience in the nation's first museum dedicated to all U.S. military veterans.

National Veterans Memorial and Museum
300 W. Broad St.
nationalvmm.org

LEARN HOW TO WEAVE
IN A WAR ARSENAL AT THE COLUMBUS CULTURAL ARTS CENTER

Tap into your artistic talent by learning how to weave, paint, or metalsmith inside a historic renovated war arsenal that is now the Columbus Cultural Arts Center. The center is a hub of artistic inspiration located in the former Ohio State Arsenal, which stored arms and weapons from 1861 until the mid-1970s. Today, the quaint brick building showcases rotating collections from local artists and student exhibitions in many mediums. Take one of the eight-week visual arts classes to learn skills in something new like jewelry-making, weaving, stone carving, watercolor painting, and printmaking. Classes are for adults over the age of 18, but the center and exhibitions are open to everyone.

Cultural Arts Center
139 W. Main St., (614) 645-7047
culturalartscenteronline.org

TIP
For those who are not ready to take the creative plunge by committing to a class, stop in to one of the weekly "Conversations & Coffee" events in the Cultural Arts Center that bring artists and art enthusiasts together in a casual and informal meet-up.

VISIT EVERY BIOME IN THE WORLD
AT THE FRANKLIN PARK CONSERVATORY

Learn about the biomes around the world at the Franklin Park Conservatory and Botanical Gardens, where more than four hundred species of plants in the greenhouses and gardens can take you on a journey from the dry heat of the desert to the exotic Pacific Islands to the rainforest all in one visit. You are likely to feel the tickle of a monarch butterfly on your shoulder during the popular Blooms & Butterflies exhibit in the spring, or you might stumble upon a wedding in the Palm House during a summer weekend visit. Wander the botanical gardens around the eighty-eight-acre complex and discover collections of species with the artistic glasswork of Dale Chihuly creatively integrated among the living plants. The Scotts Miracle-Gro Foundation Children's Garden is a two-acre odyssey of exploration with interactive activities for kids to learn about and appreciate Ohio's landscape.

Franklin Park Conservatory and Botanical Gardens
1777 E. Broad St., (614) 715-8000
fpconservatory.org

TIP

The Franklin Park Conservatory offers classes throughout the year, from cooking and yoga to watercolor painting and creating an herb garden.

HONOR AFRICAN AMERICAN HERITAGE
AT THE KING ARTS COMPLEX

The King Arts Complex in the heart of Columbus's King-Lincoln District is a creative and historical institution named for Dr. Martin Luther King Jr. The center highlights the contributions and achievements of prominent African Americans with exhibits and performances throughout the year. Walk through the compelling galleries, some of which chronicle the slave trade in America, or stroll along the hallways that feature the artistic works and history of famous African Americans. Some of the collections in the King Arts Complex spotlight the work of local artists Aminah Robinson and Elijah Pierce, who had significant influence on Columbus culture and the international arts scene. The Martin Luther King Jr. Day celebration each year is an ideal time to visit the center and experience the performances, speakers, art, and appreciation of the African American influence in the community.

The King Arts Complex
867 Mt. Vernon Ave., (614) 645-5464
kingartscomplex.com

SEE AN ORIGINAL HIGGINS BOAT
FROM WORLD WAR II AT MOTTS MILITARY MUSEUM

Higgins Boats were part of the World War II assault landings in the South Pacific, and you can see one at the Motts Military Museum in Groveport. The boat is just one of the rare pieces of military history that is preserved in the small non-profit museum built by the passionate dedication of local curator Warren Motts. Every item in the museum has a personal story since many of these relics were donated by the families of military personnel looking to find a place where the items could be protected, preserved, and appreciated. Priceless examples include a revolver used in the Civil War and a Purple Heart medal. Exhibits highlight every major war and significant military-related event in American history, including the Civil War, World War I, World War II, the Korean War, and the Vietnam War, along with collections of items from the Tuskegee Airmen, NASA, Desert Storm, and POW experiences, as well as many artifacts from the 9/11 terrorist attacks.

Motts Military Museum
5075 S. Hamilton Rd. in Groveport, (614) 836-1500
mottsmilitarymuseum.org

WALK THE STREETS OF YESTERYEAR
IN GERMAN VILLAGE

Columbus has many distinct neighborhoods reflective of the diverse cultures that originally settled the city and continue to do so, but German Village was one of the first. Take a weekend stroll along the cobblestone streets and admire the architecture of the historic homes with an ethnic flavor that has kept its original charm since German settlers arrived in the early 1800s. Stop for a cup of coffee at an outdoor café, a pastry at Pistacia Vera, a traditional hearty German meal of jägerschnitzel at Valter's at the Maennerchor, or pick up a handcrafted souvenir from the charming Helen Winnemore's gift shop. On a summer evening take a blanket and picnic basket to Schiller Park and enjoy a Shakespeare play by the Actors Theatre of Columbus on the outdoor stage. In the winter, head to German Village to admire the streets lit with luminaries during the Village Lights event that is a holiday tradition.

> **TIP**
> Columbus City Adventures leads regular tours through German Village with in-depth history and information about the area's evolution in the city at columbuscityadventures.com.

German Village Society
588 S. 3rd St., (614) 221-8888
germanvillage.com

Pistacia Vera
541 S. 3rd St., (614) 220-9070
pistaciavera.com

Valter's at the Maennerchor
976 S. High St., (614) 444-3531
valtersatthemaennerchor.com

Helen Winnemore's
150 E. Kossuth St., (614) 444-5850
helenwinnemores.com

Schiller Park
1068 Jaeger St., (614) 645-3156

GO TOTALLY ORGANIC
AT RUSH CREEK VILLAGE

In a city that is bursting at the seams with new homes, it is rare to find the kind of simple and naturally constructed community that exists in Rush Creek Village in Worthington.

Each of the fifty homes in the community is inspired by Frank Lloyd Wright's method of organic architecture in which the natural elements that surround the home become an integral part of the structure's design. That means walls, windows, and even skylights are strategically placed to embrace the outdoor landscape that is made central to the home's character. Arrange a tour of the village through the Friends of Rush Creek Village and see why this 1950s-era subdivision of minimalist Usonian homes is thought to be the largest collection in the United States inspired by renowned architect Frank Lloyd Wright.

Rush Creek Village
Located in historic Worthington, (614) 885-1247
worthingtonhistory.org

STEP INTO THE UNDERGROUND RAILROAD
AT THE KELTON HOUSE

Columbus has a number of links to the Underground Railroad, but one of the most prominent that is accessible to the public is at the historic Kelton House. The Kelton House was built in 1852 and became instrumental in hiding fugitive slaves making their way through the Underground Railroad to freedom. Get a compelling perspective of history and rare insight into the operations of the Underground Railroad by taking part in one of the historical re-enactments at the Kelton House or attending one of the regularly scheduled lectures given by local historians. The Kelton House museum and garden is available for self-guided tours during business hours. Audio guides that tell the history of the Kelton family and details about the home's interior are available for a small fee.

Kelton House
586 E. Town St., (614) 464-2022
keltonhouse.com

WALK AMONG THE GRAVES
AT GREEN LAWN CEMETERY

The 360-acre Green Lawn Cemetery is so large that it takes twenty-seven miles of narrow winding roads to access all of the areas. Opened in 1849, this is one of the oldest cemeteries in Ohio, and it houses a collection of artistic and historic treasures among its headstones and mausoleums. Unless visitors have a specific destination in the cemetery, one of the best ways to enjoy it is on foot. Historians appreciate finding the graves of prominent Ohioans like Eddie Rickenbacker, James Poindexter, Simon Lazarus, Lucas Sullivant, and James Thurber. Photographers stroll through for the quiet ambiance and endless photographic opportunities, like the mosaic stained glass Tiffany windows in the Chapel and the military section of graves often decorated with American flags. Even bird-watchers roam the Green Lawn Cemetery for the variety of resident and migrating species that can be spotted in the trees.

Green Lawn Cemetery
1000 Greenlawn Ave., (614) 444-1123
greenlawncemetery.org

TIP

Maps of Green Lawn Cemetery are available at the cemetery office near the front gates. The staff can provide insight and suggestions on locations to visit in the cemetery for first-timers.

BECOME AN ART CONNOISSEUR
AT THE COLUMBUS MUSEUM OF ART

It is easy to appreciate the plethora of historic and contemporary exhibits by walking the galleries in the Columbus Museum of Art. The collections include American and European art from the late nineteenth and early twentieth centuries, contemporary sculptures, photography, glass, wood carvings, and the world's largest assembly of works by local artists Elijah Pierce, Aminah Robinson, and George Bellows. Get creative in the Wonder Room, where the entire family can get inspired and create works of art to be displayed next to those of acclaimed textile artists. The museum is the backdrop for events throughout the year, including jazz performances, book club meetings, lectures, festivals, and social soirees. Frequent museum visitors can get a membership or stop in on Sundays for free admission.

Columbus Museum of Art
480 E. Broad St., (614) 221-6801
columbusmuseum.org

TIP
Round out a day at the Columbus Museum of Art with a bite to eat at the Schokko Café on the main floor, where the food entrees are as creative as the museum's art displays. Try creations like the appetizer of avocado toast or a crab cake sandwich made with local seasonal ingredients while enjoying the outdoor ambiance of the Patricia Jurgensen Sculpture Garden.

Intriguing contemporary art comes to life at the Wexner Center for the Arts, and exhibits at the Pizzuti Collection are guaranteed to expand your perceptions of the definition of art. Both institutions can be combined with a visit to the Columbus Museum of Art for a full weekend of artistic experience.

Wexner Center for the Arts
1871 N. High St., (614) 292-3535
wexarts.org

Pizzuti Collection
632 N. Park St., (614) 280-4004
pizzuticollection.org

GET A BIG HEAD
AT THE COLUMBUS CONVENTION CENTER

Take a selfie to outdo all selfies at the Greater Columbus Convention Center with the "As We Are" interactive art installation. A ginormous depiction of your head and face contorts on a three-dimensional, fourteen-foot-tall head in the middle of the north-end lobby. The magic happens in a tiny photo booth inside the sculpture, which scans faces with 3D points much the way human movements are created for animated movie characters. About thirty seconds later prepare for a jarring self-image as your eyes and facial features are displayed at seventeen times their real size. The sculpture was created as an art installation by Columbus College of Art & Design advertising and graphic design professor Matthew Mohr, who designed the head out of a series of swaths of ultra-bright LED screens. Go ahead, take your best shot!

Greater Columbus Convention Center
400 N. High St., (614) 827-2500
columbusconventions.com

SAY A PRAYER
AT THE PONTIFICAL COLLEGE JOSEPHINUM

As the only pontifical seminary in the United States, the Pontifical College Josephinum is a grand presence in Columbus. The international graduate and undergraduate students who live and work on campus are preparing for a life in the Catholic priesthood. While the Josephinum is a religious and educational institution, group tours are available, and there is an open house on one Saturday in the fall for visitors to get a rare look inside. Visitors who take the tour learn about the campus, theology courses, rich traditions at the seminary, St. Turibius Chapel, and the long history of the Josephinum ("house of Joseph") that started in 1888. Granted pontifical status in 1892 by Pope Leo XIII, the mission of the Josephinum is to prepare men in the seminary to serve in Catholic dioceses around the world. It is where more than 1,900 priests obtained their training. The grounds surrounding the seminary are as majestic as the structure itself.

Pontifical College Josephinum
7625 N. High St., (614) 885-5585
pcj.edu

RECONNECT WITH CHILDHOOD MEMORIES
AT THE DOLL AND TOY MUSEUM

Get ready for a big dose of nostalgia behind the doors of the Mid-Ohio Historical Museum (Doll and Toy Museum). Among the thousands of dolls and toys are treasures that date back to the early 1700s. There are one-of-a-kind displays, like a collection of thirty-eight marionettes depicting the story of Scrooge, a miniature circus collection by Charles Russell that takes up three rooms, an Alice in Wonderland collection, and even a six-foot-tall Barbie. Take a peek into the doll hospital located at the museum to see where cherished childhood toys go for restoration. The non-profit museum prides itself on its educational and cultural significance and on preserving our American children's heritage through dolls and toys. There is even a special room just for children that is filled with doll houses to encourage them to put down the digital devices and engage in simpler forms of youthful play.

Mid-Ohio Historical Museum (Doll and Toy Museum)
700 Winchester Pike in Canal Winchester, (614) 837-5573
dollmuseumohio.org

TIP

Can't get enough antique dolls? Check out The Doll Museum at the Old Rectory in Worthington, where you can find an exquisite collection of nineteenth- and twentieth-century dolls, French *bebes*, American dolls, Parian bisques, and one-inch-tall wishbone dolls.

The Doll Museum at the Old Rectory
50 W. New England Ave. in Worthington
(614) 885-1247
worthingtonhistory.org

SEE A *CRYOLOPHOSAURUS ELLIOTI*
AND COLLECTIONS OF THINGS HARD TO PRONOUNCE AT THE ORTON GEOLOGICAL MUSEUM

Visitors to the Orton Geological Museum at the Ohio State University boost their IQs just by walking through the front doors. The research facility, tucked away in the OSU Orton Hall College of Arts and Sciences, specializes in geological preservation. With more than fifty-four thousand catalogued specimens, from minerals and fossils to dinosaur relics and even a mastodon tooth, the curious can explore the earth's natural history and learn a few new words along the way. The museum's newest acquisition, the *Cryolophosaurus ellioti*, greets visitors in the lobby. It is a twenty-four-foot-long replica of an Early Jurassic dinosaur fossil discovered in Antarctica by OSU geology professor David Elliot. The free museum has the collections on display to the public Monday through Friday from 8 a.m. to 5 p.m.

Orton Geological Museum
155 S. Oval Mall at OSU's Orton Hall, (614) 292-6896
ortongeologicalmuseum.osu.edu

TIP

For an extra treat, take a tour or attend one of the regular presentations given by museum Curator Dale Gnidovec, who talks about some of the collection's prehistoric finds that are not on public display.

SHOPPING AND FASHION

FIND WHAT YOU'VE BEEN LOOKING FOR
AT COLUMBUS'S PREMIER SHOPPING COMPLEXES

Anticipate spending extra time when heading out to the shopping and entertainment complexes of Easton Town Center and Polaris Fashion Place. Both encompass shopping, entertainment, and dining in multi-level malls, outdoor shopping plazas, and adjacent stores within walking distance around the main venues.

Easton Town Center is a shopping destination on Columbus's east side with more than three hundred top retailers including American Girl, Apple, Victoria's Secret, White Barn, Tiffany & Co., and Nordstrom. Dining options range from Turkish and Indian fare to pizza, steak, and seafood restaurants. Easton features several bars, the Funny Bone Comedy Club, LEGOLAND® Discovery Center, and a thirty-theater cinema with dine-in movie options. Throughout the year Easton is the festive backdrop for outdoor concerts, farmers markets, and family holiday events.

Polaris Fashion Place is an indoor-outdoor shopping experience with nearly two hundred retailers. The complex also features specialty shops with a boutique feel as well as locally owned stores that showcase Ohio-made products. Polaris has a busy food court with traditional mall options and a wide range of neighboring sit-down restaurants featuring upscale Mexican and Chinese food, steakhouses, and the ever-popular Cheesecake Factory. The mall is popular among those getting in their steps on the weekends by mall-walking and for family events like the KidX club, with free activities for kids throughout the year.

Easton Town Center
160 Easton Town Center, (614) 337-2200
eastontowncenter.com

Polaris Fashion Place
1500 Polaris Parkway, (614) 846-1500
polarisfashionplace.com

BECOME A FASHIONISTA
AT FASHION WEEK COLUMBUS

Columbus boasts the third most fashion designers per capita in the United States outside of New York City and Los Angeles. Top fashion brands Victoria's Secret, Abercrombie & Fitch, Express, and Designer Shoe Warehouse (DSW) are headquartered in Columbus and influence the national and international fashion industry. Emerging fashion designers are groomed at nine colleges around Ohio, including the Columbus College of Art and Design (CCAD), Kent State, Cleveland Institute of Art, and The Ohio State University. With upwards of seventy percent of CCAD graduates staying in Columbus, the large local talent pool holds a strong influence in the fashion industry. The prominence of the city's fashion presence is showcased at Fashion Week Columbus, which brings together top designers with a runway show, industry mixers, and a collection of who's who in the fashion scene. Designers and fashion dreamers can all attend.

Fashion Week Columbus
fashionweekcolumbus.com

CUSTOM BLEND THE PERFECT PALETTE
AT MUKHA CUSTOM COSMETICS

Few things are more fun for a member of the female set than finding a "signature color" that is the perfect match for her skin. Mukha Custom Cosmetics is a playground of custom-blended makeup from eyeshadow and blush to lip gloss and tinted sunscreen. All of Mukha's products are blended with natural minerals and customized for each person's specific skin tone and conditions. Need a full makeover? Work with a makeup expert to create a custom palette that covers all the bases from eyeshadows to lip colors—all custom blended. Just need a little confidence boost? Try a custom, just-for-you lip gloss in the perfect shade of red with a dollop of scent from one of twenty-five essential oils in flavors like pink champagne, peach sorbet, crème brûlée, and mint julep. No Mukha product contains oil, alcohol, fragrance, dye, preservatives, paraben, sulfate, or water, so they are all good for your skin.

Mukha Custom Cosmetics
980 N. High St., (614) 294-7546
mukhaspa.com

GET LOST IN LITERARY BLISS
AT THE BOOK LOFT

Bookworms who love the opportunity to get lost in a good read need only to venture into The Book Loft in German Village to get their fix. The winding maze of thirty-two rooms offers nooks, crannies, corners, and chairs where you can settle in for a few minutes or a few hours with a good read. As one of the largest independent bookstores in the United States, The Book Loft stocks new books, best-sellers, Pulitzer prize–winning titles, and bargain books. Walk through the historic building or the home-like garden and patio for a leisurely afternoon of indulging in a favorite title or perhaps stumbling on a new one. The Book Loft hosts regular author events, readings, and presentations throughout the year for a chance to meet one-on-one with local and national authors.

The Book Loft
631 S. 3rd St. in German Village, (614) 464-1774
bookloft.com

BECOME A RHINESTONE COWBOY (OR COWGIRL)
AT ROD'S WESTERN PALACE

Every year more than 650,000 people make their way to Columbus for the All American Quarter Horse Congress, the largest show in the world for single-breed horses. The rest of the year, rhinestone cowboys and cowgirls can peruse the aisles of Rod's Western Palace and Tack Barn for everything Western, from clothing, hats, bedding, and those signature cowboy boots to saddles and spurs. As one of the top Western apparel and tack complexes in the country, customers from the weekend rider to competitive equestrians have twenty thousand square feet of retail space to explore. The store resembles a Western ranch complete with the scent of fine leather. The family-owned company still does business the old-fashioned way. It's the kind of personalized service Rod's Western Palace offered when they started in 1976, with personal attention right down to the customized detailed creases in the cowboy hats that they sell.

Rod's Western Palace
3099 Silver Dr., (614) 268-8200
rods.com

PLAY LIKE IT'S 1980
AT BIG FUN

A visit to Big Fun in the Short North should come with its own soundtrack. It is where retro is cool and the '80s are not forgotten. It is the kind of place that allows shoppers to embrace the nostalgia of childhood with vintage toys like the Spirograph, Silly Putty, Fashion Plates, and Mr. Potato Head. The concept is simple: to replicate that old-fashioned trip to the small-town mom and pop hardware store where uncomplicated toys generated simple and memorable pleasures. No two visits to Big Fun are the same because the stock of both vintage and new toys changes daily. The small space of Big Fun is packed from floor to ceiling with action figures, novelty items, books, collectibles, and forgotten toys. Try walking through the shop without saying, "Wow! I used to have one of these," at least 10 times or spotting a favorite childhood toy that your mom sold at a garage sale while you were away at college.

Big Fun
672 N. High St., (614) 228-8697
bigfuncolumbus.com

DISCOVER A NEW ARTIST
AT HAYLEY GALLERY

Inside a small New Albany art gallery is a woman who left the corporate life to pursue her passion for art and share it with the community. Hayley Gallery has the largest collection of work by emerging and established regional artists in the state. Most days you will see owner Hayley Deeter personally greeting guests who come to peruse the gallery or to buy art. Several rooms showcase a broad collection of paintings, photographs, glass art, metal and bronze sculptures, fiber jewelry, and Judaica by more than sixty Ohio artists. While the gallery is retail, it is also the backdrop for many local charity events, a venue to provide art tours for students, and an outlet for selling art made by adults with disabilities. Like a painting for your living room? Sit back on a leather sofa in one of the gallery spaces and try the artwork out on the wall to see how it might look in your home.

Hayley Gallery
260 Market St., Ste. B, in New Albany, (614) 855-4856
localohioart.com

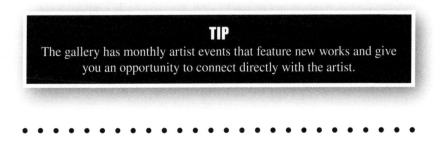

TIP
The gallery has monthly artist events that feature new works and give you an opportunity to connect directly with the artist.

121

CREATE A SIGNATURE SCENT
AT THE CANDLE LAB

Looking to create a signature scent that defines you? Do you gravitate toward outdoorsy? Clean? Bakery scents? Spice? Spa? Or a mixture of several? The Candle Lab lets customers become scent scientists and customize their own fragrances using a combination of more than 120 starting options. While candle creations are popular, scents can be made into wax melts, fragrance oils, reed diffusers, room sprays, and body lotions. Breathe deep and soak in a room scented with cake batter, chai tea, lemongrass, or lavender. Can't decide? The Candle Lab has professional "Scent Stylists" available to offer suggestions. The interactive experience takes about a half hour to select a scent, pour a candle, and create a label. It takes ninety minutes for the product to set, but all of the Candle Lab locations are in pedestrian-friendly districts with unique eateries nearby where you can grab a bite to eat while you wait.

The Candle Lab
1255 Grandview Ave. in Grandview, (614) 915-0777, ext. 3
751 N. High St. in the Short North, (614) 915-0777, ext. 2
646 High St. in Worthington, (614) 915-0777, ext. 1
459 N. High St. near the Convention Center, (614) 915-0777, ext. 700
thecandlelab.com

SHOW YOUR PATRIOTISM
AT THE FLAG LADY'S FLAG STORE

In Columbus, she is known only as the "Flag Lady," but Mary Leavitt's flag store has a long history and a deep commitment to patriotism. As one of only five flag dealers in the United States, the Flag Lady sells a wide variety of U.S.A. flags as well as custom and military flags. The Flag Lady's commitment to using products made in the U.S.A. means that each flag sold has the highest quality standards, including embroidered stars on all American flags. Leavitt first started selling American flags out of the trunk of her car in 1980 in response to the Iranian crisis so people could show their patriotism. Over the years the passion and business moved from car trunk to a basement and eventually to a storefront where the Flag Lady remains today. Just walking through the store evokes a sense of American pride.

The Flag Lady's Flag Store
4567 N. High St. in Clintonville, (614) 263-1776
flagladyusa.com

BOOST YOUR SPRING WARDROBE
DURING A SECONDHAND SHOP-A-THON

Stretching the shopping dollar in Columbus is easy with a small cadre of quality secondhand stores strategically placed throughout the city and suburbs. One More Time in Grandview was one of the first consignment clothing stores in Columbus, opening in 1975 with a high standard for preowned goods. One More Time now has a furniture store, One More Time Etc, and a plus-size clothing division combined with its men's, women's, and accessories store, all located on Fifth Avenue. Second Chance Consignment Boutique, also in Grandview, is a large upscale secondhand shop selling brands like Prada, Louis Vuitton, and Burberry for a fraction of the new tag price. For a wide range of current to vintage finds, check out Rag-O-Rama, which recycles clothing for every age range.

One More Time
1521 W. 5th Ave. in Grandview,
(614) 486-0031
onemoretimefamily.com

One More Time Etc
1641 W. 5th Ave. in Grandview,
(614) 486-7571
onemoretimefamily.com

Second Chance
1803 W. 5th Ave.,
(614) 488-3006
secondchancegrandview.com

Rag-O-Rama
3301 N. High St.,
(614) 261-7202
ragorama.com

BUY OHIO-MADE
PRODUCTS

Many people who visit Columbus want to take home a memento from the capital city and the movement to buy local is growing. What started as a few small shops selling Ohio-made products has expanded to specialty shops located throughout the city with some cool finds made by Ohio artists. The Ohio Statehouse Museum Shop features Ohio-made products and one-of-a-kind politically themed gifts. The Ohio History Store in the Ohio History Center is another top-stop for Ohio-made gifts like books, artifacts, and carved wooden baskets. Find handmade Ohio products like raw honey, wooden home decor, and textiles at Ohio Art Market in historic uptown Westerville. The Celebrate Local store located in Easton Town Center not only sells goods from Ohio artists but also includes items from farmers and other small businesses and has a continually changing inventory.

Ohio Statehouse Museum Shop
1 Capitol Square inside the Ohio
Statehouse, (614) 728-9234
statehouseshop.com

Ohio Art Market
30 N. State St. in Westerville
(614) 882-1015
ohioartmarket.net

Ohio History Store
800 E. 17th Ave.,
(614) 297-2300
ohiohistorystore.com

Celebrate Local
3952 Townsfair Way
(614) 471-6446
celebratelocalohio.com

GET NERDY
AT THE SOLDIERY GAMES & CARDS

At the Soldiery Games & Cards "nerd" is a compliment. The store specializes in collectible cards, miniature games, historical and fantasy games, and board games. It is also a regular gathering spot for card traders and tabletop and fantasy gamers. Take a break while perusing the aisles of more than three thousand board games to test your skills at one of ten gaming tables available for free play. The store hosts organized play for *Pokémon, Yu-Gi-Oh,* and others in addition to almost weekly *Star Wars* and roleplaying events. Stop in for a Monday Night Board Game competition, attend a Modern Magic Tournament, or join the *Pokémon* League. Players and traders can go alone or show up with a team of friends for a few hours of fun.

The Soldiery Games & Cards
4256 N. High St. in Clintonville, (614) 267-1957
thesoldiery.com

REV YOUR ENGINE
AT IRON PONY MOTORSPORTS

Embrace your inner motorsport enthusiast with a visit to Iron Pony Motorsports, one of the largest such retailers in the world. The family-owned business has been in Columbus for more than forty years fueling passion and adrenaline while helping people rev their engines. The fourteen-acre complex sells motorcycles and motorsport parts, services, and apparel. Pick up some leather accessories to look cool while riding down the highway or find a shirt to just look the part. Iron Pony Motorsports has a full dealership on-site with new and preowned motorcycles, ATVs, scooters, and utility vehicles and a rental division for short-term needs. Interested in learning how to ride for some skills to go with that new leather jacket? Sign up for lessons at the Iron Pony Riding Academy.

Iron Pony Motorsports
5370 Westerville Rd. in Westerville, (614) 901-7669
ironpony.com

FIND FUNKY GIFTS
IN UNCOMMON PLACES

Some of the most unique gifts, from cutting boards and books to hand-painted notecards, can be found in the small, out-of-the-way gift shops scattered throughout the city or tucked away in museums or neighborhoods. The small gift shops in the Columbus Museum of Art and the Wexner Center focus on art-themed items from books to prints to funky jewelry. Head for the Botanica Gift Shop & Greenhouse within the Franklin Park Conservatory for unusual botanical items like bonsai trees and fairy garden gifts perfect for gardeners. The Ohio Craft Museum is a gem for hand-crafted artisanal gifts, from glass pieces and paintings to jewelry. There is a full inventory of literary gifts at the Library Store at the Columbus Metropolitan Library downtown. The Experience Columbus Visitor Center has Columbus-themed trinkets, shirts, and gifts, along with great advice on places to visit in the city. For handcrafted gifts like scarves, quilts, and home decor that support the fifty-plus age group in Columbus, visit the Golden Hobby Gift Shop in German Village.

UNIQUE GIFT SHOPS

Columbus Museum of Art
480 E. Broad St., (614) 221-4848
columbusmuseum.org

Wexner Center Store
1871 N. High St., (614) 292-3535
wexarts.org

Botanica Gift Shop & Greenhouse
1777 E. Broad St. at the Franklin Park Conservatory
(614) 715-8010
fpconservatory.org

Ohio Craft Museum
1665 W. Fifth Ave., (614) 486-4402
ohiocraft.org

The Library Store
96 S. Grant Ave. at the Columbus Metropolitan Library
main branch, (614) 849-1008
friendsofcml.com

Experience Columbus
277 W. Nationwide Blvd., (614) 221-6623
experiencecolumbus.com

Golden Hobby Gift Shop
630 S. 3rd St. in German Village, (614) 645-8329
columbus.gov/goldenhobbygiftshop

DESIGN
A BOOK

There are still many people who love the feel and smell of a printed book. Igloo Letterpress lets those who still believe in the power of paper create their own masterpieces. Take a class on calligraphy, bookbinding, or letterpress and put the new skills to good use by making customized stationery, journals, or a book. There are even classes for kids to learn how to make an adventure journal or get instruction on learning cursive handwriting. Creatives might also want to explore workshops through the Phoenix Rising Printmaking Cooperative. For a fee, individuals and groups can learn the basics of embossing, watercolor, monoprints, letterpress, and etching from members who are experts in those techniques. The next good book that you read could be your own.

Igloo Letterpress
661 High St., Ste. B, in Worthington, (614) 787-5528
iglooletterpress.com

Phoenix Rising
243 N. 5th St., Ste. 140, (614) 444-2473
phoenixrisingprintmaking.org

FIND VINTAGE INSPIRATION
FOR YOUR HOME

Columbus has no shortage of vintage shops around town, but there are a few standouts for truly unique finds for the home. The Grandview Mercantile is tops when it comes to serendipitous finds of one-of-a-kind antiques and vintage accessories. You can almost always walk in and find the perfect complement to your home and personality, from an impressionist painting to a 1970s circular aquarium to Japanese cloisonné vases. At the Carpenter's Daughter boutique, the term "oddity" is a compliment when it comes to cool finds for home decor. The store offers a combination of vintage and contemporary furniture and antiques and almost always displays something you've never seen before.

Grandview Mercantile
1489 Grandview Ave. in Grandview, (614) 421-7000
grandviewmercantile.com

The Carpenter's Daughter
1619 W. 5th Ave., (614) 486-1600
thecarpentersdaughterfurniture.com

SHOP
FOR DESIGNER THREADS

Specialty designer boutiques are not the norm in a society overrun by large shopping malls and department stores, but Columbus has a few fashion treasures for those looking for a personalized experience. THREAD (with locations in Grandview and the Short North) carries classy collections of the latest boutique styles that are minimalist and elegant from designers like Ashley Pittman and Lizzie Fortunato. Leál boutique in Upper Arlington offers personalized service that focuses on wardrobe building with seasonal collections and trunk shows. For the contemporary vibe, Vernacular is both classic and trendy. The latest apparel from up-and-coming designers can be found at Rowe Boutique throughout the year and is featured during their fall fashion show. West Coast fashion is showcased in the clothing and accessories at Truluck Boutique in New Albany, which embodies a California look and lifestyle.

THREAD
1285 Grandview Ave. in Grandview, (614) 481-3090
930 N. High St. in the Short North
shopthreadonline.com

Leál
2128 Arlington Ave. in Upper Arlington, (614) 488-6400
lealboutique.com

Vernacular
1392 Grandview Ave. in Grandview, (614) 485-9039
177 E. Beck St. in German Village, (614) 228-2316
661 High St. in Worthington, (614) 547-7777
shopvernacular.com

Rowe Boutique
718 N. High St., (614) 299-7693
roweboutique.com

Truluck Boutique
160 W. Main St., Ste. D, in New Albany, (614) 933-3210
truluckboutique.com

DISCOVER
THE HABITAT RESTORE

One of the coolest home improvement resources in Columbus is a place that many people do not even know exists. The Habitat for Humanity MidOhio ReStore is a non-profit store that takes donations of home accessories, building materials, and appliances to resell and uses the money to build homes for those who need them. The bonus is that home improvement gurus can pick up surplus home building materials, paint, furniture, doors, electrical supplies, windows, and more for about fifty percent below retail prices. The store receives daily donations from a variety of sources like contractors, overstock inventory, and scratch and dent. Items sell fast, and it is first come, first served. Since home remodeling projects often go over budget, the ReStore should be the first place to look for items on your home improvement wish list.

Habitat for Humanity ReStore
East: 3140 Westerville Rd. / West: 240 N. Wilson Rd.
(614) 737-8673
restoremidohio.org

GET A RETRO HAIRCUT
AT LONGVIEW BARBER SHOP

Get an old-school haircut or buzz from the oldest barber shop in Columbus, the Longview Barber Shop. When the stripes first swirled outside of the Longview Barber Shop windows in 1919, the original owner, Tom Pletcher, a World War I veteran, only had two chairs. Now, as the oldest business still operating in Clintonville, the shop has six barber chairs and is still one of the cheapest cuts in the city. Walk-ins are welcome, but if time is an issue, the shop posts its wait-time in real time on its website showing the handwritten sign-in sheet. Though the shop now has a modern flare, there is a sweet nostalgia in watching the barbershop stripes swirl outside while you wait to spruce up your look.

Longview Barber Shop
3325 N. High St. in Clintonville, (614) 268-0885
longviewbarbershop.com

DISCOVER YOUR OUTDOORS STYLE
AT BARGAIN PRICES AT THE EDDIE BAUER WAREHOUSE STORE

Eddie Bauer stores feature some of the best outdoor gear on the market, but Columbus is home to the Eddie Bauer Warehouse Store and Outlet, where the in-store apparel, accessories, and gear can be picked up for a steal. The warehouse store has three areas: the Salvage Store, which has great prices but is hit or miss on selection; the Outlet Store, which carries current clothing and items that are discounted but prices are closer to retail; and the Warehouse Store, which is located in the back of the building but where the deepest discounts can be found. A dry-erase board at the front of the store highlights the weekly specials, and it is common for spontaneous specials to be announced over the intercom while you are shopping.

Eddie Bauer Warehouse Store & Outlet
4599 Fisher Rd., (614) 278-9281
eddiebauer.com

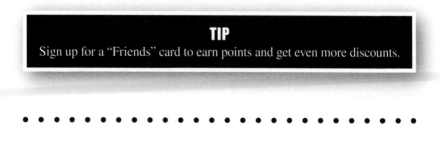

TIP
Sign up for a "Friends" card to earn points and get even more discounts.

SUGGESTED
ITINERARIES

FREE ACTIVITIES

Go to the Columbus Arts Festival, 42

Stroll Local Vendor Stalls at the North Market, 4

See a *Cryolophosaurus ellioti* and Collections of Things Hard to Pronounce at the Orton Geological Museum, 110

Picnic in an Impressionist Painting at the Topiary Park, 74

Walk the Streets of Yesteryear in German Village, 98

COLUMBUS CLASSICS

Become an Art Connoisseur at the Columbus Museum of Art, 104

Revel in Sweet Tooth Satisfaction: Experience Artisanal Ice Cream at Its Best, 2

Plan a Gallery Hop, 48

Honor African American Heritage at the King Arts Complex, 96

Watch a Broadway Show in a Restored Theatre, 40

KID FRIENDLY

Build Something at LEGOLAND® Discovery Center, 50

Savor a Candy Buckeye at the Anthony-Thomas Candy Factory, 10

Play Vintage Lawn Games at the Ohio Village, 90

Go Ape at the Columbus Zoo & Aquarium, 38

Get Charged by an Electrostatic Generator at COSI, 86

Play at the Columbus Commons, 55

SPORTS

OFF THE BEATEN PATH

DATE NIGHT

COCKTAIL HOUR

ACTIVITIES
BY SEASON

SUMMER

Join the Food Truck Fun, 5

Fill a Basket at a Farmers Market, 14

Marvel at the Butter Sculpture at the Ohio State Fair, 54

Watch Live Harness Racing at Scioto Downs, 44

Spend an Evening with the Symphony, 51

FALL

Sip Coffee with Purpose at the Roosevelt Coffeehouse, 16

Become a Fashionista at Fashion Week Columbus, 116

Try Ghost Hunting at the Statehouse, 88

Shout out O-H-I-O at an Ohio State Buckeye Football Game, 66

Tackle a Corn Maze, 72

WINTER

Cheer on the Columbus Blue Jackets, 68

Go Ape at the Columbus Zoo & Aquarium, 38

Celebrate with the City Downtown, 56

Walk the Streets of Yesteryear in German Village, 98

Design a Book, 130

SPRING

INDEX